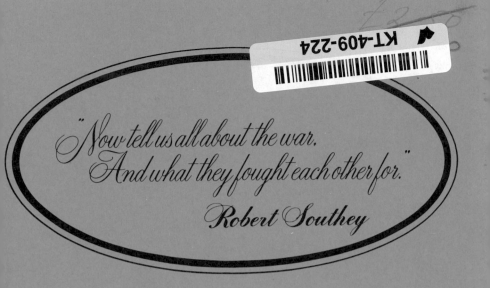

"Now tell us all about the war.
And what they fought each other for."

Robert Southey

The Battle of Salamis

In the same series

The Battle of Fontenoy
The Battle of Waterloo

Background books for wargamers and modellers

The Battle of
Salamis

Richard B. Nelson

William Luscombe

First published in Great Britain by
William Luscombe Publisher Ltd.,
The Mitchell Beazley Group,
Artists House,
14–15 Manette Street,
London, W1V 5LB.
1975

ISBN 0 86002 056 8

Phototypeset by Tradespools Ltd., Frome, Somerset
Printed in Great Britain by
Tinling (1973) Ltd., Prescot, Merseyside

Contents

◇◆◇◆◇

Illustrations

❖❖❖❖❖❖❖

I
Introduction
to Salamis

❖❖❖❖❖

In the latter years of the 6th Century B.C., the Persian
Empire, having previously overrun the former empires
of the Near East, began to extend westwards. Soon it had
swallowed up the Empire of Croesus of Lydia and the
Greek cities of the west coast of Asia Minor.

In the first decade of the 5th Century B.C., the Greeks
of Asia Minor revolted against Persian rule and, aided
by the homeland states of Athens and Eretria, took and
burnt Sardis, the former capital of Croesus, now the
Persian administrative centre in Asia Minor.

Persian reaction was swift, and the revolt was sup-
pressed by strong land and sea forces. Following the
suppression of the uprising, a punitive expedition was
mounted against Athens and Eretria, in 492 B.C. Not
for the last time, the weather aided the Greeks, and the
invasion fleet was wrecked rounding the rocky promontory of Mount Athos. Two years later a second punitive
expedition was launched, this time coming across the
central Aegean.

Eretria fell by treachery, and the inhabitants were

shipped off into slavery. However, despite similar attempts to gain Athens by treachery, the Athenian land forces, their only ally being the small city of Plataea, caught the Persians at a disadvantage, and crushingly defeated them at Marathon.

For ten years there was no further Persian attempt against Greece. Internal revolt in Egypt, and a change of King, delayed the reckoning, but revenge for Marathon remained a Persian ideal. Territory was absorbed, with the subjugation of Thrace and Macedon, which brought the frontiers of the Persian Empire ever closer to Greece. Finally in 481 B.C. the new King of Kings, Xerxes, demanded fire and water in token of submission from the free Greeks. The general rejection of this demand made the invasion planned for the next year inevitable.

In western Asia Minor the Persians built up a huge army, supported by a fleet drawn from all the maritime nations under their control, and backed up by supply and logistics arrangements of formidable scale and efficiency. Astute propaganda placed the number of troops at millions, the ships at thousands, and there were, as a result, many voices in Greece, including the oracle of Apollo at Delphi, who were counselling submission.

But the free cities of Greece prepared to defend themselves, and under the overall leadership of Sparta sent a fleet and army to block the approaches to Central Greece at Artemisium and Thermopylae respectively. In a series of engagements the Greek fleet, though suffering considerable losses, nevertheless held the Persian ships at bay, and the odds against them were further reduced by a fortunate storm, which created havoc among the Persian ships, too numerous to find shelter along the restricted beaches of the area of Cape Sepeia.

At Thermopylae, however, the Persians had betrayed to them a path which enabled them to outflank the defenders. Most of the Greeks got away, while the Spartan king Leonidas, with 300 Spartans and other troops, made a heroic last stand, and fell with all his men. The way was now open for the Persian army to enter Central Greece. The Greek fleet, in danger of being isolated, withdrew from the Artemisium position, and concentrated in the straits of Salamis, near Athens, while the Greek land forces prepared to defend the Isthmus of Corinth.

The Persian objectives now appeared to have been achieved. Athens was taken and burnt in revenge for Marathon. The Greek fleet at Salamis was reported to be in danger of disintegration, with a serious dispute over strategy which was likely to see an irremedial break between the Athenians and the Peloponnesian contingents. The Persians had only to attack and disperse their numerically inferior enemies, and the way would be clear for them to outflank the Isthmus defence line and bring the campaign to a triumphant conclusion.

Yet when the Persians attacked the Greek fleet at Salamis, they were utterly defeated in one of the greatest naval battles of history. The Persian invasion force, with its seaborne supply route now unprotected, was forced to retreat, and in the following year a Greek army drove the remnants of the Persian troops out of Greece for ever.

It was perhaps inevitable that the great victory at Salamis should become for the Greeks, and for their cultural heirs, a symbol of Freedom Triumphant over the Forces of Tyranny. The present book, tracing the history of the campaign and of the Battle of Salamis, and using wargame techniques, reconstructs the course of the fighting and illuminates a number of points of obscurity. At the same time a number of paradoxical points come to light, such as the large Greek contingents which fought loyally and effectively on the Persian side.

So the reality is perhaps more complicated, and the participants neither so black nor so white as represented in legend. The importance, however, of the victory won by the ships of Greece in September, 480 B.C., remains.

2
The Ships
at Salamis

◆◇◆◇◆◇◆

In the decades prior to the Persian Wars, there had been a revolution in naval architecture. For centuries sea warfare had been fought with galleys, but these had been powered by rowers seated on one or at most two levels, with oars having their thole pins in ports in the ships' sides. The invention of the *trireme* permitted a ship having the same overall dimensions as a two level galley a 50 per cent increase in oar power, with a consequent increase in speed and in endurance. So rapid was the acceptance of the overwhelming advantage which the trireme had over other ships that the fleets which fought at Salamis were exclusively composed of this type of vessel.

The details of the construction and appearance of the trireme are by no means certain, and this is not the place for a discussion of the various theories. Interested readers should refer to the bibliography, where they will find listed works giving the differing points of view, and reviewing the ancient evidence. The details given here represent the most probable and generally accepted reconstruction of these vessels. The illustrations show three-view scale reconstructions of Phoenician and Greek triremes.

The trireme was in excess of 100 ft. long, but narrow in the beam. The hull itself was no more than 12 to 14 ft. at the widest, but the upper banks of oars were carried on an outrigger frame, rectangular in plan, which was about 18 ft. wide. It was the invention of this outrigger which had enabled the trireme to be developed, and an extra bank of oarsmen to be carried in a vessel no larger than its predecessors. The total length-to-beam ratio was about 8:1, similar to that of a modern destroyer, and a displacement of about 50 tons is probable. The ships were of shallow draft, and were normally beached at night.

The appearance of a trireme was distinctive. The bows bore a large bronze ram under the waterline, and to counterbalance this the stern was swept up in a graceful curve like a scorpion's tail. The ram itself took the form sometimes of an animal's head, such as a wild boar, sometimes a simple spike, sometimes three superimposed points. Above the ram the bows terminated in a hornlike stem, the purpose of which was probably to fend off an enemy in ramming to prevent too deep a penetration. If this happened, the ramming ship might have difficulty in backing clear, and be fatally involved with the sinking ship. In the bows was a deck, upon which fighting men could stand, with protective screening up to a height of 3 or $3\frac{1}{2}$ ft. The bows were normally decorated with a large pair of eyes, sometimes

Fig. 1. Exterior elevation of a Phoenician trireme. The high sides are the most noticeable feature, with permanent wicker screens and above them shields. In the stern can be seen the standard carried by all Phoenician vessels, with the disc and crescent symbol.

Fig. 2. Interior elevation of a Phoenician trireme. The disposition of the rowers is clearly indicated (see also Fig. 4). A central gangway is suggested at the level of the thalamite *oarsmen, and the majority of the marines would have been stationed here, ready to move to the attack. In the stern the helmsman can be seen, sitting in an elevated position and controlling the two steering oars.*

painted, sometimes a carved feature of either wood or marble fixed to the vessel's side.

The distinctive upcurved stern bore a pair of steering oars, one each side, controlled by a helmsman sitting centrally, and steering the ship by means of short handles set at right angles to the main steering oars. The modern type of rudder was not to be invented for many centuries, but the steering oars of the trireme are unlikely to have been inferior in performance.

Between bow and stern was the outrigger and the main hull, housing the rowers. At the period of the Persian Wars, there were probably 150 rowers in total, three banks of 25 rowers per side. These rowers were all free men, and certainly in Greek fleets, their pay was the main cost incurred in operating the trireme. Each rower had an oar, as well as his own leather cushion to sit on and a leather thong to bind the oar to the single vertical thole pin. This method of securing an oar to the thole pin may still be seen in Greek waters.

The centre of the vessel was taken up with a gangway, and on either side of this gangway sat the lowest bank of rowers, called *thalamites*. The thalamites sat at an interval of 2 cubits (3 ft.) from each other – in other words with just sufficient space for one man to operate an oar efficiently.

Slightly higher than, and outboard of, the thalamites sat the second bank, called *zugites*. They were staggered in the intervals of the thalamite oarsmen, and their

Fig. 3. Plan of Phoenician trireme.

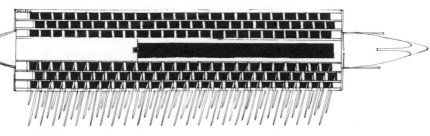

thole pins were 1 cubit (1½ ft.) higher than those of the thalamites.

Again slightly higher than, and outboard of, the zeugites sat the third bank, or *thranites*, who were held to be the most skilful oarsmen. Again staggered in the gaps between the zugite oarsmen, the thranite oars emerged from the outrigger 2 cubits directly above the thalamite oars. All three banks of rowers had oars of similar length, about 14 ft., of which 11 ft. or so were outboard. The angle at which the oars met the water was correspondingly greatest therefore with the thranite oarsmen.

Fig. 4. Section of Phoenician trireme showing arrangement of oarsmen. Top : the thranites ; middle : the zugites ; bottom : the thalamites.

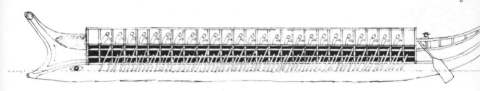

Fig. 5. Greek trireme – elevation. The more racy appearance of the Greek trireme is evident in this reconstruction. Under battle conditions the rowers would be concealed by leather or canvas screens suspended from the topmost frames.

It would only be under battle conditions, when high speed was called for, that all three banks would row together. Rowing was very hard physical work, particularly under the Mediterranean summer sun, and the length of time which a rower could row continuously was limited in consequence. It was normal for only one bank of oarsmen in a trireme to be rowing, with the other two resting, so that only one bank of oars was showing and in operation. At a date well after the Persian Wars, a Greek admiral with plenty of ships, but scanty crews, bluffed his opponent into avoiding battle by manning three times as many ships as he had rowers for. His rowers manoeuvred their ships into line of battle, changing banks from time to time to give the illusion of full crews, and the enemy, believing their opponent to have been substantially reinforced, declined action.

Fig. 6. Greek trireme – plan.

The sides of the trireme were open above the lowest level of oarsmen, and leather shields could be fitted, through which the oars protruded, to give protection against spray and waves. The topmost oarsmen could however be seen, and a different type of screening had to be provided to protect them in battle from missiles. The practice of fleets varied. Greek ships carried the frames of the vessel above the level of the outrigger, and curved them outboard slightly. From these frames were suspended leather or canvas screens,

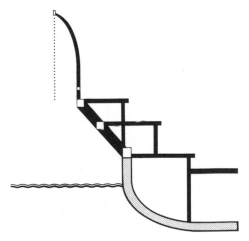

Fig. 7. Section of Greek trireme, showing the outcurvings of the frames to accommodate the side screens used in battle.

called *parablemata*, as protection against missiles, when the ship was going into action. Phoenician vessels had permanent wicker screens, painted in contrasting colours, and topped with open frames from which shields were hung. The effect of this was that a Greek trireme had under normal circumstances an apparent freeboard of 5 ft. or so, compared to the 10 ft. of the Phoenician, and had therefore a much more racy appearance. Phoenician vessels had, however, similar hull lines and rower dispositions to the Greeks, and were certainly not inferior in performance.

While the main power for the trireme, particularly under battle conditions, was provided by the rowers, a single large square sail was carried on a mast stepped somewhat forward of the centre of the ship, about at the centre of gravity. This sail was used to supplement and spell the rowers, but both mast and sail could be struck, and indeed were normally left ashore before the vessel went into battle.

Triremes were normally brightly painted and decorated, and were adorned with carved wood in places. In particular, a ship would have a figure, similar to the later figurehead, which represented its name, and would also have a symbol of nationality. In the Athenian fleet this took the form of a golden figure of Pallas Athene, while Phoenician vessels carried a standard on the stern with a disc and crescent. Ship names, at least in the Athenian fleet, always had a female form, and were generally 'lucky' sounding.

The captain of the trireme was the *trierarch*. In Greek fleets he was usually a wealthy citizen, who was given command of the ship as an honour. In return for this he had to obtain a crew for the vessel (paid for by the state), and himself pay for the upkeep of the ship during the campaigning season. The qualifications for the Athenian trierarchs at Salamis are given in the so-called 'Troezen Decree', and are: 'Possession of Land and House at Athens, age 59 or under, and having sons born in wedlock.' The trierarchs were chosen by the Generals, who were the 10 elected military and naval commanders for the year, and were obviously men of substantial property. Certain wealthy Athenians even bore the whole cost of a trireme for the Salamis campaign, voluntarily undertaking a financial burden several times greater than that of the ordinary trierarch.

It is obvious that the qualifications for the trierarchy did not include nautical experience or knowledge of naval warfare, and the trierarch's second in command, the *kubernetes* or helmsman, who was the most experienced professional seaman aboard, was therefore an

Trierarch (captain of Trireme)

Four ship's officers:

Kubernetes (helmsman) Keleustes (in charge of rowers)

Proreus (bow officer) Pentekontarchos (junior officer)

 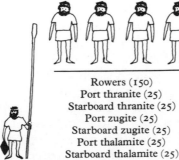

Auletes (fluteplayer to give time to rowers)

Sailors (4)

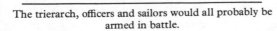

Rowers (150)
Port thranite (25)
Starboard thranite (25)
Port zugite (25)
Starboard zugite (25)
Port thalamite (25)
Starboard thalamite (25)

The trierarch, officers and sailors would all probably be
armed in battle.

Marines or fighting troops (40)

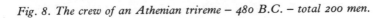

Fig. 8. The crew of an Athenian trireme – 480 B.C. – total 200 men.

19

important officer. His station was in the stern, to steer the ship and control the two steering oars. On an Admiral's ship the kubernetes would assume at least some of the functions of a chief of staff, and should not be regarded as a mere steerer.

In charge of the rowers was the *keleustes*, who was assisted by a flute player to give the time. Modern films show rowers being given the stroke by drum, which is unhistorical.

Other officers included the *proreus*, or bow officer, possibly responsible for the non-rowing gear (sails, anchors etc.) and the *pentekontarchos*, or junior officer.

Separate from the naval crew were the marines, the fighting troops. At this period most ships seem to have carried about forty, and they were probably stationed in the central gangway area, since there was not room on the foredeck for them all. When their ship rammed another, they would go pouring over the foredeck and the *apobathra* (see page 28) on to the enemy vessel. (Marine types are fully described later in the sections on fleets).

The rowers have already been described, but it is worth stressing that rowers in the ancient world were normally not slaves, but free men, often as keen to extort the proper rate for the job as any trade unionist.

Crews included, in addition to the men so far detailed, sailors for the handling of sailing gear and anchors, under the proreus, and such essential functionaries as a carpenter (*naupegos*). The grand total of all crew is normally considered to have been about 200 per ship.

While the trireme was the main battleship of all fleets at this period, other ships were present at Salamis. The obsolete *pentekonters* and *triakonters*, ships with rowers on one or two levels instead of three, and with fifty and thirty rowers respectively, were found in small numbers, but were not capable of meeting triremes in battle on equal terms.

The pentekonter had in fact been the standard battleship of all fleets, but was now relegated to scouting

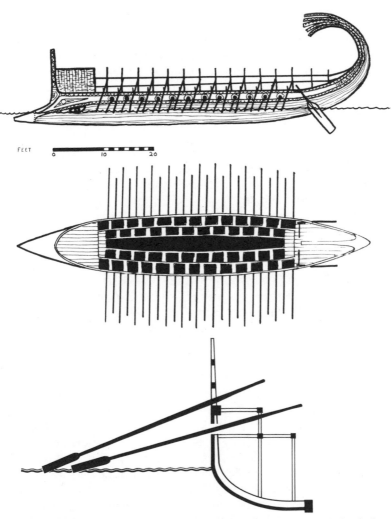

Fig. 9. *Greek pentekonter. This reconstruction of a double-banked pentekonter resembles the trireme in general appearance, but is half the length and lacks the outrigger and thranite oar bank.*

As with the trireme, a single mast and square sail is carried. This is stowed along the centre line of the vessel when not in use.

The upper oars are carried on the gunwale, and above this level the frames of the ship continue to support an open framework.

As with all Greek ships, the pentekonter would be brightly painted and highly decorated.

and support duties. On the Greek side, one or two small States who had not the resources or manpower to supply a trireme, contributed pentekonters. Originally having 25 oarsmen per side, each with one oar, and all on the same level, the pentekonter was now probably a shorter vessel, with the same number of rowers disposed on two banks, and it is such a vessel which is illustrated in Fig. 9.

The standard Greek warship features are present in the pentekonter, with the upper bank of oars having thirteen oars in total, with their thole pins on the level of the gunwale. About 18 in. below them, and staggered in the gaps, are the lower bank of oars, twelve per side. The rowers for the lower bank sit inboard of those on the higher. Both banks of oarsmen use oars of about the same length, but it will be noted that the lower bank have a larger proportion of their oars inboard.

To some degree, both the 'two bank' pentekonter and the trireme represent different lines of development from the original single-banked pentekonter. Once the advantages of multiple banks of oars had been discovered, 100 oars could have been fitted into the original pentekonter hull length, and such a ship would have had a clear advantage in speed and power over the original pentekonter. There is no firm evidence for such a vessel, which we could call a hekatonter (from the Greek for 100), but it forms a logical 'missing link' between the pentekonter and the trireme. Assuming that it existed, it must fairly swiftly have been superseded by the trireme, carrying the multiplication of banks to a logical conclusion within the constructional limits then obtaining, and only being made possible by the invention of the *parekseiresia* or outrigger.

While the trireme became the standard battleship, there remained a need for a lighter class of vessel. For these duties a double-banked pentekonter possessed important advantages over the old single-banked type, and thus probably became the norm. The development of the pentekonter was probably paralleled by the triakonter, the latter vessel merely having 30 instead of 50 oars, 8 in the upper and 7 in the lower banks of each side.

The development of warships may thus be summarised as follows:

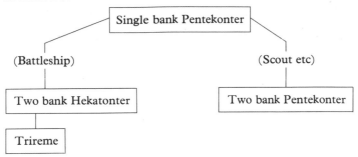

In addition to the fighting ships, the Persians were accompanied by large numbers of store ships, carrying supplies for both fleet and army. At this period of history, such supply vessels would have been impressed merchant vessels, with a likely carrying capacity of 100–150 tons. The typical merchant ship was a beamy vessel, with a hull form somewhat reminiscent of half a walnut shell. It relied upon a single square sail for propulsion and had no oars, although two-masted vessels, and vessels with some type of fore-and-aft sail (both of which will materially have improved handling capability), were to be found within a relatively short period later.

The method of supply used by the Persians seems to have been that the supply vessels all began the campaign loaded, and accompanied the fleet, with their supplies being expended as required.

Assuming as an arbitrary figure that the Persian army and fleet totalled 400,000 men, which is a reasonable estimate, accompanied by 70,000 animals, and taking the total weight of supplies (other than those obtained locally) required as 2 kilos per man and 5 kilos per animal, this gives a total requirement for the army of 750 tons per day, and for the fleet of 400 tons (army and fleet both calculated at 200,000 men). This is the equivalent of five large vessels for the army and three for the fleet.

23

Over a four month campaign, Xerxes thus needed 960 shiploads of supplies, though this need not imply 960 ships, as there could have been a shuttle service to and from a base like Doriscus, with each ship making two or three journeys. However, supplies seem to have been stored in the ships awaiting discharge, which was obviously the most convenient way of arranging matters, even if it did create a slow turn-round of shipping.

3
Strategy
and Tactics
at Salamis
◇◇◇◇◇◇

The limitations of the trireme governed the strategy
available to a fleet of the period of Salamis, and in
particular limited the strategic options available to
Xerxes in his invasion of Greece. The trireme had
something of the dimensions and accommodation standards of a very crowded railway carriage, with no
restaurant facilities, and no sleeping accommodation. It
therefore required to be brought to land at frequent
intervals, so that the crew could go ashore to cook meals
and to sleep. Wherever possible, therefore, an admiral
would put ashore at night, and often also at midday.

Unlike more modern warships, however, the trireme
required no complicated harbour facilities – although
often housed in large and elaborate bases in practice –
and on campaign was simply beached stern to shore.

As cruising speeds were of the order of three knots, it
thus follows that a Greek or Persian admiral would,
after a voyage of thirty miles, be seeking a convenient
sheltered beach with good water supply, safe from
enemy attack by land or sea. Of course under exceptional

circumstances a fleet might undertake longer voyages without a stop, but this would be at the risk of extra crew fatigue.

An ancient fleet was therefore restricted to a fairly close radius of friendly territory, unless in sufficient strength to overawe any defending force in hostile territory. If faced with a hostile fleet it required a temporary safe base as close as possible to the probable scene of action, so that non-essential equipment could be left behind when ships cleared for action (this included mainmast and mainsail). The crews would also be as rested as possible when battle commenced.

Thus such more modern naval activities as blockade or commerce raiding were normally ruled out for an ancient fleet, unless that fleet had access to nearby friendly bases.

When two fleets met, the tactics which they might adopt would depend upon which school of thought they favoured: Ram or Board. The advocates of boarding aimed to grapple the enemy in close combat and overwhelm them by the fighting power of their marines. The advocates of ramming sought as their target the enemy ship, not its crew, and aimed to sink or cripple their opponents by superior skill, speed and handiness.

In the Salamis campaign the Greek ships, whose speed and manoeuvrability were restricted by the relative inexperience and lack of training of their rowers, were forced to rely on boarding tactics, in which indeed the formidable Greek *hoplite* gave them a decided advantage. The Persian squadrons, and especially the skilled ships from Ionia and Phoenicia, were always seeking a situation where superior skill could be brought to bear.

The tactical requirements of a Boarding fleet were simple. The ships must keep close together, they must keep their bows towards the enemy, if necessary by backing water, and they must keep their flanks protected. The interval between ships is, however, unlikely to have been less than somewhat over one length, or say 150 ft.

Unless there had been some such interval as this, it would have been impossible for any ship to turn without running foul of a neighbouring ship or ships, and causing serious and possibly crippling damage.

A Boarding fleet would naturally adopt a line abreast formation, with the flanks protected by land (e.g. in a narrow strait), or by being bent back or refused. At Artemisium the Greeks carried refusal of the flanks to the extreme of forming a defensive circle prows outwards, like a herd of musk-ox, and variants of this type of formation included half circles, with both flanks refused and resting on one stretch of coastline.

The types of soldiers used at Salamis are described in the chapters on the individual fleets, but included, besides heavily armed infantry, missile-men of various kinds. Most formidable of these were javelin-men, armed with javelins, shield and sword, because they could fight effectively hand-to-hand as well as at a distance. However their use in Greek fleets was restricted by social factors – anyone who could afford the equipment would fight as a hoplite, and anyone who could not was required to row. The main Persian weapon was the bow. In any case, since they had to cast from a stationary position, the effectiveness of javelins on shipboard was limited.

Perhaps least affected of missile-men were archers, the commonest type of missile troops. At Salamis the Persians carried large numbers of bow armed troops – thirty per ship. Given the restrictions on space to deploy bowmen, and the extensive protection against archery provided by the types of sidescreen, the effectiveness of the bow was restricted to individual targets. Most promising would be enemy helmsmen or captains, who would be exposed in the stern, but would present difficult marks, with both firing and target ship moving in at least two dimensions at speeds of up to 8 knots.

The only special equipment carried by ships intent on boarding were appliances called *apobathra* (Fig. 10): these appear to have been gangways, fitted at the forward ends of the parekseiresia or outrigger. Possibly about 12 ft. long and 2 ft. wide, they could be lowered on to an enemy vessel after ramming, to facilitate boarding by the marines. Alternatively they could be used for disembarking for instance on a defended shore.

Fig. 10. Impression of the bow of a Greek trireme, showing the probable position of the apobathra, *the boarding gangways which Greek ships rigged before going into battle, situated at the front of the* parekseiresia *or outrigger.*

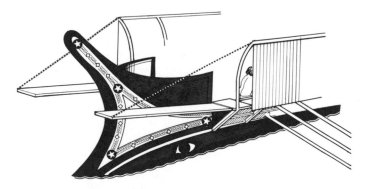

Apart from rigging *apobathra*, clearing for action largely consisted in stripping the ship of all unnecessary equipment, the main items left behind being mast and sails. However, in later times, and possibly in this period as well, triremes took into battle an auxiliary sail which could be used for escape, should it be necessary to take to flight.

A fleet relying on the ram, rather than fitting extra equipment, tended towards light and handy ships, and placed a premium upon skilled crews and expert seamanship. At the time of Salamis this trend had not gone as far as it did in later times, when the Athenian navy reduced the number of marines to ten hoplites and four archers. All ships still carried the same number of marines, whatever tactics they intended to use.

The emphasis on speed did not necessarily mean that a ramming fleet was manoeuvring at high speed constantly. Under normal conditions a fleet would not exceed 3–4 knots, to avoid overtiring the rowers, although if required a trireme with a good crew could probably maintain at least 8 knots for 20 minutes or so. The evidence suggests that ramming was a skilled operation, and that excessive speed was likely to be a disadvantage. With the specially designed bronze ram, a moderate impact would be sufficient to open a hole in the side of a lightly constructed wooden ship like the trireme; if the ram took place at speed, it could be expected that the ramming ship would become inextricably entangled with its victim. Furthermore, a ship charging at speed could not easily change course, and might overshoot the target, doing itself crippling damage in the process.

The epitome of ram tactics was the *Diekplus*, the 'Through-And-Out-Sail', which was a speciality of both the Phoenician and Ionian captains in Xerxes fleets. The purpose of the Diekplus was to break up the line abreast formation of a fleet relying on boarding, and the ships carrying it out would assume a line astern formation. The Diekplus was carried out as follows (see Fig. 11). The leading ship would aim for a gap between two enemy vessels. When approaching the gap, the helm would be put hard over, and the ram would be swung into the side of one of the two enemy ships. The object was not however to penetrate; with both ships moving the ram and stem of the ramming ship would slide down the side of the target ship, shearing off the oars and creating injury and chaos among the rowers. Further damage to the steering gear might also result. The ramming ship's oblique position would protect its own vulnerable oar banks. The helm movement of the rammer, and the impact on the rammed ship, would make both vessels swerve.

Now the rammers could exploit the situation. The lead ship would already be picking up way again and coming round behind the enemy line, ready to attack the vulnerable sides and sterns. Furthermore the supporting ships, following up at a rapid pace, could attack

Fig. 11. The Diekplus *in action. The Black ships are in line astern formation, and are carrying out a* Diekplus *on the White ships, which are in line abreast. Black 1 has just wiped out White 3's port oarbanks, and both ships have veered to port, with White 3 crippled. Black 2 has elected to follow Black 1 through the gap between White 2 and White 3. Had White 4 not turned to port, Black 2 could itself have turned to port and rammed White 4 in the port beam. The White ships are all turning inwards to close the gap, but in doing so, tend to expose their sides to the advancing Black column, and Black has already succeeded in forcing a mêlée in which the faster and handier Black ships have an overwhelming advantage. Note that if White had had a second line Black 1 would have been a sitting target!*

the enemy vessels on either side of the gap or could pass through the gap themselves.

The Diekplus was easily countered. The defenders simply put a second line of ships behind the first. Any ship which tried to carry out a Diekplus on the first line would thus find itself broadside on to the second line, and in an ideal position to be rammed. Provision of a second line could however fatally shorten the overall frontage of the Board fleet, rendering the flanks vulnerable, and restoring the advantage to the Ram fleet.

In the particular conditions of the Salamis campaign, the very large numbers of ships deployed made the Diekplus a practical impossibility. However, Greek numerical and skill deficiencies compared to the ace Persian squadrons made it essential for them to hold narrow waters, where the Persian superiority in numbers could not be brought to bear, and where the Ionian and Phoenician squadrons would not have the sea-room required to take full advantage of their superior speed and manoeuvrability.

4
The Persian
Fleet

◆◇◆

It is paradoxically the case that the Persian fleet at Salamis was not Persian at all and was in fact half Greek! In fact it was provided by the various subject races of the Persian Empire with naval traditions, each separate tribe or nation sending its own contingent under its own officers. Overall command was however exercised by Persian admirals, and a contingent of ethnic Persian marines was embarked on each ship.

The numbers of the individual contingents provided by the various nations is given by Herodotus, and is as follows:

Phoenicia	300 triremes	The best contingent with fastest ships
Egypt	200 ,,	
Cyprus	150 ,,	
Cilicia	100 ,,	
Pamphylia	30 ,,	
Lycia	50 ,,	
Dorians	30 ,,	Greeks of Asia
Carians	70 ,,	

Ionians	100	„	Greeks of Asia
Aeolians	60	„	Greeks of Asia
Islanders	17	„	Greeks
Hellespontines	100	„	Greeks
Thracians	120	„	Greeks
Total	1,327		

Aeschylus also gives a total number of ships which can either be interpreted as 1,000 or 1,207; the latter is the more probable and corresponds to the number given by Herodotus, less the Thracian Greeks, who joined Xerxes' forces after the muster at which Herodotus numbers the contingents.

Both Aeschylus and Herodotus count only triremes in these figures, as being the only battleships, but there were also large numbers of supply and scouting vessels, including large numbers of the now obsolete pentekonters.

Now, while these figures are individually and in total credible as being within the Persians' power to have built, several points argue that the actual number of ships which Xerxes could count upon in battle was probably considerably fewer.

First, because the accuracy and detail of the numbers available to the Greek historians argues that they derive from some official source – and probably an official Persian source. Under the political circumstances prior to the battle of Salamis, and the campaign leading up to it, Xerxes can be expected to have given as large a figure as he could for his fleet, but equally one which was credible, if inflated.

Second, because the cost of an ancient warship was always much less than the cost of paying its crew, most ancient naval powers had many more ships available than in commission, and the Persians are likely to have been no exception.

Third, because by the time of the battle of Salamis, the Persian fleet did not have an overwhelming numerical superiority over a Greek fleet which did not much exceed 300.

Fourth, because the Persian strategic preparations for the campaign included the construction of two pontoon bridges over the Hellespont which required over 600 triremes and other ships, and Herodotus gives no indication of where these were obtained from.

Fifth, because the fleet was commanded by four Persian admirals, one, Achaemenes, a full brother of Xerxes, commanding 200 vessels from his Satrapy of Egypt; another, Ariabignes, commanding the Ionian and Carian contingents (170 ships), and the remaining two commanding the rest of a fleet consisting apparently of 1,207 or 1,327 vessels. Since two of the admirals had commands of about 200, it is illogical that the other two admirals should have had such dissimilarly sized divisions.

It is therefore suggested that the Persian navy in the campaign of 480 B.C. consisted of four 'Fleets' of about 200 vessels each, containing a variable number of subordinate contingents. The additional numbers given by the sources represent vessels which were in fact levied for the campaign, and which were trumpeted forth by the Persians, but which were not manned, and were only used for the construction of the Hellespont bridges. The attraction of this is that the majority of the ships required for the bridges come from the subject nations nearest to the Hellespont, which of course would have made for ease of assembly of the components.

The four fleets are, then:

1. The Fleet of Phoenicia
This fleet was provided by the maritime Semitic cities of the Syrian and Palestinian coasts, chief of which were Tyre and Sidon. The king of Sidon was the senior national commander – his name is given in Greek form as Tetramnestus. Mattan was the King of Tyre.

It is probable that the Fleet of Phoenicia is the same as the 207 outstandingly swift ships which are mentioned by Aeschylus, as Herodotus confirms that the Phoenicians were the swiftest and best ships in the Persian array,

The Persian Fleet – Conjectural Estimate of Numbers, Campaign of 480 B.C.

Fleet	Component Contingents	Number in Herodotus	Warships at start of Campaign	Warships Supplied for Pontoons	Total 'National' Marines	Total Persian Marines	Total Crews	Overall Commander	Losses at Artemisium (all causes) Ships approx.	Losses at Salamis Ships approx.	Total after Salamis Ships approx.
Phoenicia	Tyre Sidon etc.										
	Total	300	207	93	2070	6210	41,400	Prexaspes or Megabazus	50	85	72
Egypt Cyprus	Egypt	200	200	—	2000	6000	40,000	Achaemenes	100	—	100
	Cyprus	150									
	Cilicians	100									
	Pamphylians	30									
	Lycians	50									
	Total	330	200	130	2000	6000	40,000	Megabazus or Prexaspes	150	30	20
Ionia	Dorians	30									
	Carians	70									
	Ionians	100									
	Islanders	17									
	Aeolians	60									
	Hellespontines	100									
	Thracians	120									
	Total	497	200	297	2000	6000	40,000	Ariabignes	50	85	65
Grand Total		1327	807	520	8070	24,210	161,400	—	350	200	257

and among them the Sidonian contingent was out-
standing.

The Phoenician ships carried marines who were
equipped with helmets of Greek type, linen corselets,
rimless shields, and javelins. The shields will have been
round, and about 2 ft. in diameter. The linen cuirass was
a quilted garment which could vary in length, with
elbow length sleeves. The Phoenician preference for
javelins tends to confirm the effectiveness of these
weapons in naval fighting, as the typical weapon of the
Syrian peoples was the bow.

If we take the Phoenician contingent as 207 ships, or
about that number, we must assume that the total levy
(given by Herodotus) was 300, of which about 100 ships
were solely required for incorporation into the pontoon
bridges.

The Persian commander of the Fleet of Phoenicia
was either Prexaspes or Megabazus.

2. *The Fleet of Egypt*

The Egyptian fleet was 200 ships strong, which is
both the strength given by Herodotus, and the actual
inferred strength levied. Egypt was a populous country,
and would have had the least manpower problems, so all
the ships available could be manned; equally any ships
for the pontoons which were brought from Egypt would
have had the furthest distance to come.

The Egyptian marines showed themselves to be the
most effective in combat against the Greeks, and were
relatively heavily armed, with large wooden shields,
large spears, and axes. Again, many of them had the
quilted linen corselet. The shield could cover the entire
body down to the feet, and probably had a square cut
bottom and round top.

The commander of the Egyptian contingent was
Achaemenes, who was a full brother of Xerxes, and was
Satrap of Egypt. The importance of the Egyptian
command to the Persians, and the trouble which had
in the recent past been caused by revolts there, can be

gauged by the highly connected individual it was thought necessary to appoint to ensure it stayed loyal.

3. The Fleet of Cyprus

This is the name given for convenience to the consolidated unit formed by the nations of the coast and islands of Southern Asia Minor. The numbers given by Herodotus are:

Cyprus	150 ships
Cilicia	100 ships
Pamphylia	30 ships
Lycia	50 ships
	350

To make this fleet the same size as the others we must postulate about 200 fully manned warships levied and 130 old ships also levied for the pontoon bridges.

The marines for the Cypriot and Pamphylian vessels were equipped in Greek fashion, while the Cilician marines had helmets, rawhide shields, and javelins. The Lycians wore cuirasses and greaves, with caps crowned with feathers, and were armed with bows and javelins.

The Commander of the fleet of Cyprus was either Megabazus or Prexaspes – whoever did not command the Phoenicians.

The fleet of Cyprus bore the brunt of the first two days fighting at Artemisium, and appears largely to have been eliminated as a force by the time of Salamis.

4. The Fleet of Ionia

This is again a convenience name given to the fleet commanded by Ariabignes (who was killed at Salamis), and consisted, according to Herodotus, of the Ionian and Carian contingents, 170 in number. It is postulated that in fact the command of Ariabignes comprised the following ships:

Dorian Greeks of Asia	30 ships
Carians	70 ships
Ionian Greeks	100 ships
Island Greeks	17 ships
Aeolian Greeks	60 ships
Hellespontine Greeks	100 ships
Greeks of Thrace	120 ships
	497

Of this total of 497 ships, it is postulated that nearly 300 were to be used for the pontoons, while 200 were fully manned warships. This fleet was recruited from the areas nearest to the location of the pontoon bridges, so that it provided most of the ships required for this enterprise.

All the marines in this fleet had Greek style equipment, and their ships will also have been similar to Greek ships in type. Because of their maritime traditions, they provided a fleet which was ship for ship at least the equal of the best free Greek vessel. Initially some of them were reluctant to fight against their free brethren, but in the

Fig. 12. Persian Marine. The dominant races of the Persian Empire were the Medes and Persians. While they were two distinct races, and had distinctive dress, when fighting both races wore the Median dress. The Persian style of garments consisted of a long skirt or kilt, reaching to the feet, and a loose tunic with baggy sleeves, which was retained for ceremonial duties, but was not a practical proposition on campaign.

The style of dress illustrated here is the Median, consisting of trousers and a tunic with tighter sleeves than the Persian, both highly decorated and embroidered in bright colours. The headdress is the tiara, *a loose cloth garment resembling a balaclava helmet in principle.*

There is some dispute over body armour. Persians are said to have worn iron scale armour, but this is not shown in most of the contemporary illustrations, and does not appear in many battle descriptions. It appears most likely that the armour was often worn, but under the tunic — practical in a hot climate, and not apparent to the eye. At any event, the absence of a helmet, combined with a less effective shield, made Persian troops inferior to Greek hoplites, whatever the degree of body armour.

The shield, of distinctive shape, was made of wicker. Offensive weapons were a spear, shorter than the Greek spear, and a bow of composite type, carried in a combined bowcase and quiver slung from a belt. A dagger or sword was also carried.

fighting at Salamis they fought at least as well as the Persians.

Herodotus records that there were 30 Persian and Sakae marines on board each ship, in addition to the national marine contingents. The total crew for a trireme was about 200, of which about 150 were rowers, and perhaps 40 in total marines. This gives an average of 10 national marines and 30 Persian and Sakae marines per ship. The chart at the end of this chapter summarises the strengths of the various contingents at different stages of the campaign.

While a fighting fleet of 800 ships maximum represents a considerable reduction from the grand total of 1,200 or more in the original sources, it was still twice the size of any fleet which the Greeks could be expected to muster against it. What is more, in the Phoenician fleet the Persian command had a contingent which could be expected to get the better of any Greek force in water where there was space for manoeuvre, while the Egyptian and Persian marines may have been thought at least the equal of the Greek hoplite. The most recent experience of fighting the mainland Greeks, at Marathon, may have encouraged the Persians, because although they had lost the battle, their Persian and Sakae troops had broken the Athenian centre, and the battle was lost by the defeat of their flanking subject levies.

So far two functions of the Persian fleet have been considered: fighting the enemy fleet, and providing the vessels for the pontoon bridges to enable the army to cross from Asia to Europe. A third function, perhaps most important of all, was to provide a screen behind which the supply vessels, on which the Persian land army depended for its survival, could shelter.

The land army probably consisted of about 150,000 fighting troops, with numerous supporting units. Some of the more favoured units had extensive baggage and camp followers. Depending upon the number of cavalry and baggage animals and other factors, such as availability of grazing, this force could easily have needed

Fig. 13. Sakae Archer. The Sakae were Scythians who were favourite troops with the Persians at the period of Salamis, as supports for their own Persian and Mede infantry. The basic dress was similar to the Median dress, brightly and intricately-patterned trousers and tunic. The most noticeable feature was the tall pointed hat, illustrated on numerous monuments, and apparently made of leather. There was no body armour.

Offensive weapons consisted of a composite bow, carried in a bow case and quiver similar to the Persian one, and the sagaris, *the typical Sakae axe. This differed from modern axes in having a transverse head.*

The Sakae were a Bactrian tribe, and were renowned horsemen, but were apparently equally effective as footmen. They were the invariable auxiliaries of Persian troops in the actions of the Persian Wars. The moustache is attested from contemporary Bactrian art!

750 tons of supplies per day. If this could not be obtained by foraging, and this was not likely to be possible in Greece, such a daily requirement represents about 7,500 animal loads, or could be carried in a few cargo vessels. Four or more cargo ships could have carried the army's entire daily supply needs, and a total of 300 could operate a shuttle service to magazines in the Hellespont area or Thrace, which would have been ample to keep Xerxes' force supplied.

The events of the campaign showed that the army could readily maintain itself from its own resources for a week or so, arguing that there may have been 70,000 pack animals with the force. But after Salamis loss of the screen provided by the fleet was sufficient to force the army to withdraw immediately.

Finally, the Persian commanders must be considered. To Greek tradition of course the Persians were an effete and unathletic people, solely formidable because of their immense numbers and great wealth. Their luxurious habits and ridiculous trousers alike made them contemptible. As a result Xerxes in particular gets endowed with characteristics more suited to a tyrant of melodrama.

The reality, as usual, was somewhat different. The Persian commanders at this date were all members of the Royal or a few aristocratic families, and the complexity of their relationships are confused by the fact that the Persian kings in particular had numerous wives and concubines. No less than ten full or half brothers of Xerxes took part in the campaign, and the efficient planning of the campaign, if it was somewhat monolithic, still argues competence in the high command. Leadership was both vigorous and personal – Ariabignes, killed at Salamis, was one of Xerxes half brothers – and in the following year both Mardonius, the Satrap designate of Greece, and his cavalry general Masistius, were killed leading cavalry charges.

The character of Xerxes hinself is worth study, but is difficult to ascertain. At the time of Salamis he was probably about 40. From Persian inscriptions he appears as a centraliser and a somewhat puritanical religious autocrat and reformer. Ahura Mazda may be God, but Xerxes is second, and the rest nowhere. In Herodotus he has the typical Persian love of natural beauty and of agriculture and horticulture – paradise is the Persian word for garden – and while capable of generosity on a large scale, he could also show his displeasure violently and unpredictably. As far as the present campaign is concerned, this will have made him unforgiving toward failure, and unwilling to take notice of contradictory advice, once he had made up his mind on a course of action.

5
The Greek
Fleet
◆◆◆

The Greek fleet in the Salamis campaign was initially
very much inferior to the Persian, not only in numbers,
but also in the skill of the crews and performance of
ships. The Greeks were in general outclassed both by
the Phoenician and Ionian fleets, and most of their
strength, the new Athenian navy, had only been in
existence a few years.

The individual contingents in the Greek fleet may be
classified as follows:

1. The Athenian fleet
The total Athenian fleet is given by Herodotus as 200
ships, of which twenty were manned by Athenian
colonists from Chalkis. It was not only the largest,
but also the newest fleet, and owed its very existence to
the fortunate discovery of a rich new vein of silver in
the Athenian silver mines at Laurium, and to the per-
suasive powers of Themistocles, who succeeded in
persuading the Athenians not simply to share this
money out among the citizenry, but to use it to create a

fleet. Prior to this, both Aegina and Corinth had completely outclassed Athens at sea.

The total of 200 Athenian ships, of which 180 had Athenian crews, seems to represent the largest commitment of manpower of which Athens was capable at this period. In the campaign of 479 B.C., when Athens put a large army in the field, there had to be a substantial reduction in the size of the fleet.

A recently discovered inscription, the so called 'Troezen inscription', allegedly gives the mobilisation orders for the Athenian fleet for this campaign; it is more probable that what it gives is the later Greek idea of what the orders were, for there are numerous problems.

The most immediate problem is the number of marines per ship. According to the Troezen inscription there were ten hoplites and four archers to each Athenian vessel, the hoplites being chosen from those between 20 and 30 years of age. Now this number of marines is more appropriate to the later Athenian fleet, when the emphasis was not on boarding, but on manoeuvre, and large numbers of marines were a liability. It is more likely that Athenian marines were as numerous as those of other Greek fleets at this period, and a total of about 40 is required per ship. This incidentally gives a total hoplite manpower with the fleet of 180 × 40 or 7,200, which represents about 75 per cent of the Athenian available manpower, of the hoplite class.

The commander of the Athenian fleet was Themistocles, who is the man who planned the strategy of the campaign from the Greek side, and who is generally awarded most of the laurels. The Athenian military system was based on the ten tribes into which the people were divided for administrative purposes; each of the tribes elected a General (who might serve by land or sea) every year for a term of one year. While, therefore, Themistocles had colleagues, he himself was the effective commander of the Athenian fleet.

Themistocles was at this time in his late 40's, and his

Fig. 14. Greek Hoplite. This is a typical Greek hoplite, who formed the fighting crew of the Greek ships which fought on both sides at Salamis.

The essentials of his equipment are a bronze helmet – that illustrated is the type known as Corinthian, although variants were worn, some exposing more of the face, some with hinged cheek pieces. All had, however, the large crest of horsehair.

The cuirass is of the type known as 'composite', and consists of a bust shows a stocky figure with a short beard. He was the leading exponent at Athens of development of the fleet, and was thus associated with the more radical democracy, as it was the lower classes who would benefit from any naval expansion. The conservative landowners and well-to-do classes, who provided the hoplites for the Athenian army would tend to oppose him in this matter. It was solely through Themistocles' efforts that Athens had a fleet at all.

Themistocles reputation comes down to us largely through his political opponents, and he is even, in one late source, accused of human sacrifice! He was certainly a character who was not averse to devious dealings, and

---

leather or canvas backing to which metal scales are sewn; this is laced down the front. The shoulder pieces are fixed to the back of the cuirass and are brought forward over the shoulders and laced to the front of the cuirass. From the cuirass, at waist level, a skirt of leather flaps (called pteruges or feathers) protects the lower part of the body.

The shins are covered by thin metal Greaves; these had a cloth backing and were designed to snap into place on the shin, so that no lacing etc., was necessary.

The shield was bronze or bronze-faced on wood, convex, and about 3 ft across. Circular or sometimes slightly oval in form, it was carried on the left arm by a band in the centre of the shield, through which the forearm was thrust up to the elbow. A handgrip inside the rim for the left hand provided control. The anchor motif here shown has no particular nautical significance, but was the blazon of Sophanes of Dekelea, a famous Athenian fighting man of the period. The figure has his arm hanging straight downwards; in battle the left forearm would be brought up to a horizontal position, rotating the shield through 90°.

Athenians had individual shield blazons, but some other states had standard insignia on their shields. The Spartans had the Greek letter Lambda (initial of Lacedaimon) and the Sicyonians similarly used the Sigma. The symbols of Corinth and Aegina on coins were Bellerophon, the winged horse, and a tortoise respectively, but it is not always possible to assume that the symbol on coins was the same as that used on shields, even if a common shield blazon was used.

The offensive weapons of the hoplite consisted of a sword, carried in a scabbard supported on a baldric going over the right shoulder, and a long spear. On land hoplite tactics involved dense close order formations of spearmen – the phalanx – but at sea more individual fighting tactics had to be employed.

there are several stories of him receiving and taking bribes in the course of the campaign.* However, the attitude of Greeks to such practices was not quite that of our modern age, and if Herodotus may be believed, those who received bribes included not only Themistocles' Corinthian counterpart, but the highly respected Spartan admiral Eurybiadas. As will be seen, Themistocles' inclination to clandestine affairs was the main factor precipitating the battle of Salamis.

2. *The Spartans and their Allies*

This division contained the following contingents:

Sparta	16 ships
Corinth	40 ships
Megara	20 ships
Aegina	30 ships
Sicyon	15 ships
	121 ships

Although the Spartans provided only a small naval contingent, as the foremost military power of Greece they were accepted as supreme commanders by all parties. The Spartan admiral Eurybiadas accordingly took precedence over the other contingent commanders, including the commander of the largest contingent, Themistocles. It would in practice have been impossible for old established naval powers like Aegina or Corinth to serve under an Athenian.

The Corinthians played an important part in the battle. Their commander, Adeimantus, was at this time a fairly young man (he had several children born in the years following Salamis), who appears in Herodotus as the main adversary of Themistocles, advocating a contrary strategic policy, based upon withdrawal to the Isthmus of Corinth.

*One of these bribes amounted to several hundredweight of silver. A recent historical novel depicts Themistocles receiving this amount in a purse, which he describes as 'agreeably heavy'!

This of course, while representing the immediate short term interests of Corinth (and the other Peloponnesian states) would have been fatal to the Grand Strategy of the alliance.

3. Ships from the Argolid

This contingent was supplied by cities which had been allies of Argos (which was neutral in the war) prior to her recent defeat by Sparta.

Epidauros	10 ships
Troezen	5 ships
Hermione	3 ships
	18 ships

Troezen was of course the city where most of the Athenian refugees were despatched after the fall of Thermopylae.

4. Western Aegean Islands

This contingent comprised

Eretria	7 ships
Styra	2 ships
Keos	2 ships
Kythnos	1 ship
	12 ships

Most of these ships were provided by states on the island of Euboea.

5. Corinthian Colonies

Ambracia	7 ships
Leukas	3 ships
	10 ships

These Corinthian colonies are in the western approaches to the Gulf of Corinth, on the trade route to Sicily.

6. Other ships

A total of seven ships, comprising six deserters from the Persians and one ship from the Greek colony of Kroton in Italy, manned by volunteers.

The total of the Greek fleet is given by Herodotus as 380 ships, but the contingents enumerated above amount only to 368. To reconcile the numbers it is suggested that he has omitted a squadron of 12 vessels which were retained at Aegina to protect the island, and did not join the main fleet.

If the figures are thus reconciled, the figure of 380 ships does not represent the total size of the Greek fleet at any particular point in the campaign, but is an aggregate of every vessel that formed part of the fleet at any stage in the season's operations.

At Artemisium the Greeks disposed of not more than 325 ships, and of course suffered losses in the fighting there. It would appear that while some further ships were mustered at the port of Pogon, and joined the fleet between Artemisium and Salamis, they did not entirely make up the battle losses at Artemisium, and the fleet at Salamis was at about the level of 310 ships suggested by Aeschylus.

The casualties at Artemisium were heavy – we are told that half the Athenian fleet was damaged. If however we assume that most of the damaged ships were repaired fairly quickly, and that total losses were of the order of 20 per cent, we get the following figures for the Greek fleet at Salamis, which are, of course, approximate only:

Athenians and allies	160 ships	(all from Artemisium)
Sparta and allies	101 ships	(21 from Reserve fleet)
Argolid	16 ships	(5 from Reserve fleet)
Western Aegean	11 ships	(1 from Reserve fleet)
Western colonies	11 ships	(11 from Reserve fleet)
Others	7 ships	
	306 ships	

While an approximate calculation only, this figure is useful in tending to confirm the possible scale of loss at Artemisium, and the probable relative proportions of the various squadrons. The main feature is that the relative importance of the Athenian contingent declines. The Athenians were of course a new naval power, and would have lacked the reserve of ships which could be patched up and put to sea if necessary by more established powers. Because the Greeks retained command of the battlefield at Artemisium, any ships of theirs which were total losses will still have had their crews intact, and these could have manned reserve ships if they had been available.

It might at this stage be appropriate to make mention of the 'Might Have Beens': ships which could have swelled the Greek numbers. Corcyra, the modern Corfu, sent a fleet of 60 ships, which would have represented a considerable reinforcement to, and indeed the second largest contingent in, the Greek fleet, if it had arrived. Unfortunately the Corcyrean fleet never succeeded in rounding Cape Malea in the southern Peloponnese, either because of unfavourable weather, as they claimed, or because they did not try very hard – as everybody else claimed!

An even larger potential reinforcement was the fleet of Syracuse in Sicily, a full 200 triremes, and the Greeks had made overtures to Gelon, the ruler of Syracuse, to seek his alliance. However, Gelon had proposed unacceptable terms, possibly because he was faced with the danger of a Persian-inspired Carthaginian invasion. In fact he destroyed the Carthaginian invasion force at the battle of Himera about the time that Salamis was won.

All the Greek vessels were similar in design, and the crews were also basically similar. Recruited largely from their own cities (in contrast to later Greek practice, which tended to rely on mercenary rowers), the oarsmen were all free men, and in the case of Athens and certain other cities, fully franchised voters as well. The marines were from the higher social classes, and were in the main equipped with the hoplite panoply. Total numbers per ship were similar to the Persian fleet, 200 men, of whom about 40 were fighting men and 150 rowers.

The command structure of the Greek fleet may be inferred from our sources. The Spartan admiral Eurybiadas was acknowledged by all as supreme commander, but under him each contingent commander seems to have had an equal voice, whether he was Themistocles with 200 ships behind him, or some admiral with five or fewer vessels. In the end concerted action had to be by consensus, as there was no way of ensuring that a contingent would obey orders if it did not desire to. It may be noted that the Greek words for 'to obey' and 'to be persuaded' are similar. The result was that any Greek Council of War might degenerate into a violent argument, with everyone shouting at once. This was in strong contrast to Persian councils, where the subordinate commanders were definitely seen and not heard, or rather gave their opinions in strict order of seniority, and then only when asked for them. Of course the strategy of the campaign called for the Persians to believe that the Greek command was split immediately prior to Salamis, and some of the apparent dissension may have been skilfully contrived; Themistocles at least would have been capable of it.

6
Events
leading up to
the Battle
◆◆◆◆◆

The Persian invasion plan was neither complicated nor subtle; Xerxes instead relied upon the efficient deployment of overwhelming strength. The Persian background planning was very thorough and on a massive scale.

The plan itself called for a large army, supplied from magazines in friendly territory and after that by an accompanying fleet of storeships, and accompanied by a large fleet, to traverse the northern shore of the Aegean, enter Greece, defeat any opposition and establish the Persian Satrapy of Greece.

The essential points of the plan can be seen from Fig. 15 (see page 54). Thrace was part of the Persian Empire, and Macedon, under its King Alexander (Alexander I, not to be confused with Alexander the Great), could be relied upon to cooperate with Xerxes. (Alexander was a master of the double or treble cross who spent the campaign assuring both sides that his sympathies were really with them). Both Thessaly and Boeotia were known to be ready to declare for the Persians as soon as the army entered their territory. It

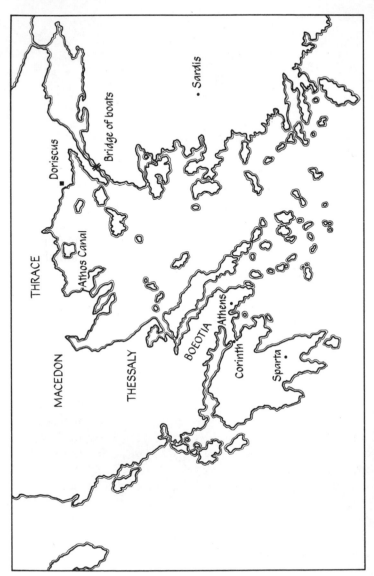

Fig. 15. The Persian strategic plan, 480 B.C.

must have appeared to the Persians that the campaign might be chiefly one of logistics.

The first requirement was the establishment of supply magazines to feed the army while on the approach march. A large magazine and base were established at Doriscus in Thrace, and further bases were set up in Thrace and Macedon. Doriscus itself was intended to be the main assembly point for the expedition, and had ample grazing and water supplies.

To reach Doriscus the army had to cross the Hellespont. To facilitate the crossing the Persians constructed two huge pontoon bridges, using over 600 old warships. The bridges were destroyed once in a storm, but were successfully established at the second attempt. The building of these bridges was in fact a highly practical act, as the alternative would have been to ferry the entire army across using the fleet, which would have presented immense difficulties, particularly in shipping the many thousands of animals accompanying the force.

Prior to the Marathon campaign a Persian fleet had been wrecked attempting to round the Athos peninsula. Xerxes had therefore had a canal dug across the base of the peninsula so that the fleet could avoid a repetition of the previous disaster.

Finally, every device of propaganda was employed to ease the passage of the army into Greece. No secret of the massive scale of the preparations was made, so that the intended victims might be intimidated into offering no resistance. Greek spies caught in the Persian Camp were escorted anywhere they pleased, allowed to make what notes they wished, and courteously sent home again. Lavish bribes were sent to open and secret sympathisers in Greece.

By July 480 B.C. the Persian army and fleet were poised to enter Thessaly.

The Greeks tried two defence plans, both with the intention of meeting the enemy as far forward as was possible. The one advantage which the Greeks had, both on land and at sea, was that their forces were very difficult to defeat, provided that their flanks could not be turned. The mountainous nature of Greece provided several positions where a smaller force might hope to hold off a larger one.

The first of these positions was the Tempe Pass, a narrow gap between Mounts Olympus and Ossa, and forming the boundary between Thessaly and Macedon. In Spring 480 B.C. the Greeks sent a force of 10,000 hoplites to hold this Pass, and prevent the enemy even entering Thessaly.

The Greeks on arrival found a number of disadvantages to the Tempe position. First, and most serious, it was not the only practicable pass, and the Greeks could not be expected to hold all the passes. Second, the Thessalians themselves, who provided the best cavalry in Greece, were of doubtful loyalty and could be expected to change sides. The Greek Generals were reluctant to hold a position where they might suddenly be attacked from the rear by their 'friends'. Third, there was no satisfactory position for the Greeks to station a fleet, allowing the Persians the opportunity of landing forces in Thessaly behind the backs of the force holding the pass.

Despite the political and strategic advantages, therefore, of meeting the enemy as far forward as possible, the Greeks withdrew from the Tempe passes after only a short occupation.

By the time the Persians entered Thessaly unopposed, the Greeks had decided to hold the land positions of Thermopylae together with the channel between the mainland and the island of Euboea. This position was far superior to the Tempe position. The pass at Thermopylae was very narrow, and although it could be turned, 5,000 troops were sent to hold it and these were thought ample to hold the various approaches. While the loyalty of the Boeotians might be suspect, there were a number of loyal cities in the Thermopylae area.

But the main advantage of Thermopylae was the naval position based on the beaches of Artemisium in

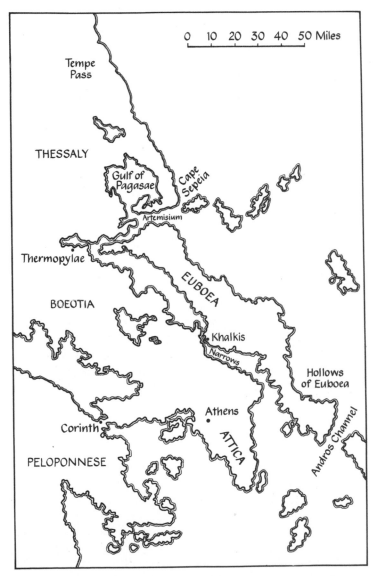

Fig. 16. The Greek plans for defence, 480 B.C.

northern Euboea. Between the Tempe pass and the southern tip of Euboea the coast was mainly rocky and hostile, with few small harbours. With the Greeks holding the only good beaches in the channel between Euboea and the mainland, the Persian fleet could either enter the straits and use the less adequate beaches opposite Artemisium, many of them badly sheltered and the whole not permitting a proper concentration of the fleet, or they could attempt to go round Euboea and turn the Artemisium position from the south.

The great advantage of this double position for the Greeks was that it kept the Persian fleet and army separate, while the Greeks were in communication. If the Greeks could only hold this would start to create supply difficulties for Xerxes army, since the supply ships were with the fleet.

While the Persian army began to mass in front of the Greek forces at Thermopylae which were commanded by King Leonidas of Sparta, the Persian fleet also moved. Because of its superiority in numbers, the Persian admirals tried both options available to them. The main fleet took up position opposite Artemisium, while a substantial detachment (200 ships according to Herodotus) were sent to circumnavigate Euboea (possibly a detachment of the Fleet of Cyprus).

At this point the elements favoured the Greeks, because a north-easterly storm blew up. The Persian armada, many of whose ships were at anchor because the beaches were full, was caught and many ships were driven ashore and destroyed or damaged. More serious, the flanking force was caught off the Hollows of Euboea, and completely destroyed.

The Greeks had about 270 ships available at Artemisium, with a further 53 Athenian ships stationed in the Narrows, guarding against any flanking move by the Persians. Assuming that the storm losses indicated by Herodotus are correct, the Persians probably now had about 500, having lost the flanking force and more from the main fleet, although news of the loss of this force had not yet reached the admirals.

The fighting off Artemisium fell on three separate days. On the first day the Greeks sent out a force late in the day to engage the enemy. (The number is unknown, and it may not have been the whole fleet). This force was attacked by a superior number of Persian ships, but having formed a defensive circle, prows outwards, and been surrounded by the enemy, engaged in a boarding battle, in which it had considerable success, taking thirty enemy ships. The prisoners included a Prince of Cyprus.

The first day's fighting off Artemisium sounds like an engagement between parts only of the main fleets. The Greek defensive circle as described by Herodotus sounds too well drilled a manoeuvre for the whole fleet (and would have had a circumference of about 5,000 yards and been a mile across). We may rather infer that it was a trial of strength between a Greek squadron including Athenian ships (one of whose captains received the prize for valour), and a Persian squadron including Cypriot vessels. Since the Persian anchorages were spread out, the Greeks could engage part of their fleet in the late afternoon, knowing that darkness would intervene before the main Persian strength could be brought into action.

Before fighting was resumed the Greeks received reinforcements from the 53 Athenian ships which had been guarding the narrows, and the Persians received word of the loss of their flanking force. The second day's fighting took the same form as the first, a Greek raid on an isolated Persian squadron (in this case Cilician) and a quick withdrawal at nightfall before the Persians could respond.

While this sparring had been going on off Artemisium, the Persian land forces had been engaged in furious fighting, making a series of frontal assaults on the Greeks in the pass at Thermopylae. The apparent inactivity of the fleet must have made a strong contrast, for the Persian admirals determined to take the initiative on the next day.

Accordingly about midday the entire Persian fleet

attacked the Greeks, who fought with their backs to their anchorage off the north shore of Euboea; the relatively late start to the battle was probably caused by the long delays in getting all the Persian vessels collected from their scattered individual anchorages.

The battle that ensued was on the same scale as the later action at Salamis, but was inconclusive. The Greeks must have had over 300 ships available, the Persians at least 500. This assumes that although there had been casualties over the previous two days fighting in the Persian fleet, some of the storm damaged ships had been brought back into commission.

The Persian tactics were to try to outflank the Greeks, but they were foiled by the Greek position near their own base, and probably the Greeks had refused the flanks of their line. At any event the fighting took the form of a mêlée, in which the more numerous Persians found themselves tending to get in each other's way, and the heavily armed Egyptian marines had the most success, capturing five Greek ships.

At the end of the day the Persians withdrew to their bases, leaving the Greeks in technical command of the area of the battle. Both sides had, however, suffered very heavily – half the Athenian ships had been damaged to a greater or lesser extent.

The action was not however renewed, because in the course of that night a message came that the Persians had taken the Thermopylae position and that Leonidas was dead. A practical route through the mountains had been betrayed to the Persians and the 10,000 Immortals, the best troops in Xerxes force, had brushed aside the defenders of this route and come down in Leonidas' rear. The way to central Greece and Athens was open, and for the fleet to stay in the Artemisium position any longer would be too suicidal.

During the night the Greek fleet therefore withdrew down the channel between Euboea and the mainland.

The Greeks now had several possibilities open to

them. It was clear that all mainland Greece as far as the Isthmus of Corinth must fall to the Persians, Athens having been evacuated, and the Peloponnesians were in favour of withdrawing to the Isthmus, fortifying it (which was indeed in hand) and making no further effort north of that line. The cities north of the Isthmus naturally wanted at least some further action, and could legitimately claim that there was no suitable position for the fleet supporting the Isthmus line which would not see the seaward flank turned by the Persian fleet. And if the fleet was not in being, then the Persians could use their own ships to land troops behind the Isthmus defences. The Greek reserves for the fleet were mustering at the port of Pogon; they, and the survivors of Artemisium, were directed to Salamis, just off the coast of Athens. While Salamis was held, the Persian fleet could not pass on to flank the Isthmus of Corinth; to take Salamis involved entering the narrow strait between the island and the coast of Attica, and meeting the Greek ships in waters where they could expect to enjoy every superiority.

It was an unharried withdrawal to the Salamis position. The first essential for the Persians was to re-establish contact between fleet and army, and ensure that the army was resupplied. Once this had been done, the army moved to occupy Boeotia (which swiftly came over to the Persian side, as expected) and Athens, and when the beaches by Athens were in the Army's control, the fleet came down to occupy them.

It was a deserted Athens which was occupied by Xerxes. After Artemisium and the fall of Thermopylae, the entire population was evacuated in the ships of the Athenian fleet and by every other possible means. Most of the refugees went to Troezen, by Pogon, where the reserve fleet was mustered; some went to Aegina, the island in the middle of the Saronic gulf, and some went to the island of Salamis itself. Only a few men stayed behind and prepared to defend the Acropolis against the invaders.

The Peloponnesians were still demanding a retreat to the Isthmus, but on the insistence of the Athenians and other central Greek states, backed up by the threat that they would unilaterally desert, the Allies agreed eventually to concentrate at Salamis, and the reserves moved there from Pogon. Meanwhile the Persian army occupied Athens, and the fleet was based on the beaches of Phaleron and the harbours (not yet developed) of the Piraeus. It was now about the end of August, and Xerxes sent back a message announcing his success to Persia.

But the campaign was by no means over. The Acropolis itself was stubbornly defended by the few Athenians who had not left with the majority of the population. The main approaches had been barricaded with wooden barriers, which the Persian archers succeeded in setting on fire with fire arrows, but their initial success could not be exploited because the defenders rolled large rocks down on anyone trying to assault the breach. It took some time before the Persians found a way in by climbing a precipitous cleft, in the north face of the Acropolis, which was not even guarded.

Even with Athens completely in his hands, Xerxes was still no further forward. The Greek land forces were busy fortifying the Isthmus of Corinth, but the Persians could not advance to attack them while the Greek fleet remained in being in the Salamis strait. Nor did his admirals relish the prospect of entering the strait after their experiences fighting the Greek fleet at Artemisium.

The solution which Xerxes initially determined on was entirely in character with the solutions he had previously ordered for the problems of the Hellespont and the Athos peninsula; he simply determined to construct a mole from the mainland across to the island of Salamis, down which his army could march to subdue the defenders. The reduction of Salamis would leave the way open to the Isthmus, and there would be no sheltered position for the Greek fleet to hold, preventing the Persians from outflanking the Isthmus defences with their own fleet.

The Persian engineers accordingly began their work in the hot September sun, but even the shortest route involved a mole of about 1,500 yds. in length, which might be expected to require up to 1,000,000 cu. ft. of material, and which had to be positioned in the face of active intervention by the Greek fleet. For about the first two hundred yards of the mole, the Persians would be able to defend it with archers on the shore. As the construction extended beyond the range of troops on shore, it could only be protected by troops on the mole itself, and these could not be too numerous without hampering the workmen and/or requiring the mole to be built impossibly wide. The work accordingly languished, despite a project to extend it rapidly by using merchant vessels as a pontoon bridge, evidently in the middle where the depth is greatest.

As September passed it became increasingly obvious that a strategic stalemate had been reached; at least to the Persians. Xerxes position was indeed difficult. He had already announced the successful occupation of Athens, and to prolong the campaign would create political difficulties, quite apart from those which might be the result of too long an absence from the centre of the Empire. We do not know, but it is likely that the Persian plan had assumed the campaign would be concluded in one season. If so, and Xerxes held on, he would run out of supplies for his forces and suffer serious losses in consequence. The main hope of the Persians must have been that their continued presence and occupation of Attica would place an intolerable pressure on the Greek alliance – and indeed it must have placed a serious strain on Athenian self-control to see the daily devastation of their homeland. In their dealings with the Greeks, the Persians had always encountered disunity and mutual distrust sooner or later, and Persian diplomacy was skilled in exploiting such dissension.

If, as seems certain, the Persians were getting intelligence reports from the Greek camps on Salamis, it must have given them hope, because there appeared to be a serious dispute about strategy in the Greek command. The Greeks living south of the Isthmus felt that they were too far forward and were seriously exposed in the Salamis position. They were arguing for a retreat to the Isthmus. The Athenians led the opposite party, pointing out that this proposal was nonsense, and would result in the fall of all Greece. The Athenians were even known to be threatening to withdraw unilaterally, embark all their population on their ships, and set off to Italy to found a new Athens there.

One can therefore imagine the Persian experts on Greece assuring the high command that Greek unity would not long survive, and it must have seemed like a vindication of all their forecasts when a message was received from none other than the Athenian Commander, Themistocles, indicating that the Greeks were planning to break out from the Salamis position by night, and that the Athenians were preparing to desert the alliance.

7
The Terrain

It is appropriate at this stage to describe in more detail the area of the conflict, because the terrain itself has a considerable bearing on the course of the battle. The limits of the terrain governed the options which were open to the commanders on both sides.

The general strategic area can be seen in Fig. 17. The Persians were in command of the area round Athens, but whilst raiding the rest of Attica, had probably not occupied it in force. Thebes had, of course, declared for Persia and was now actively on the Persian side. Megara had not yet been occupied, although there were some threatening Persian moves in that direction.

The island of Salamis sticks out like a sore thumb in the centre of the map, incapable of being ignored by the Persians. The Greek land forces behind the Isthmus are about a day's sail away to the west, the majority of the Athenian refugees at Pogon a day to the south. It is clear that any Persians advancing beyond Salamis would have to move a considerable way before reaching an area of any importance. If such a move was made they

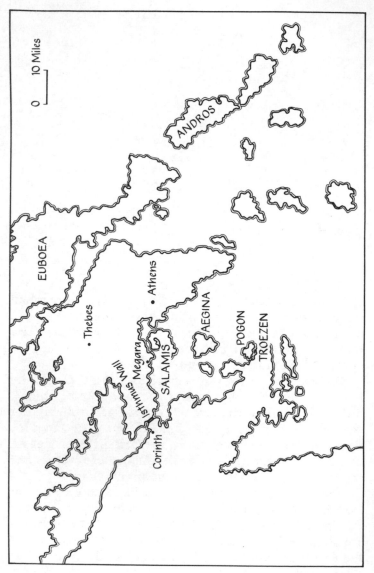

Fig. 17. The strategic situation at Salamis.

could not prevent damaging Greek naval activity against targets in the immediate vicinity of Athens.

The area in which the battle took place is illustrated in greater detail in Fig. 18. The majority of the Persian vessels occupy the Phaleron area, with some holding the natural harbours of the Piraeus promontory. The Greek fleet holds three separate beaches on the east side of the island of Salamis, within the straits. The main beaches, the largest, were held by the main body of the fleet, including the Athenians; it is suggested that the Corinthian squadron held the northernmost beach and the Aeginetan squadron the southern.

It is worth stating at this stage that there have been changes in sea level since the period of the battle; certainly the relative positions of Greece and Turkey have altered by about 100 yards. The maps are based upon modern shorelines. The most likely alterations which were present in 480 B.C. are that some parts of the straits were shallower. Along the intended course of the mole suggested in Fig. 18, the modern depth is mainly between one and two fathoms (6–12 ft.), and parts are shallower. In ancient times a lower sea level in this area might have exposed a reef near the mainland end of the mole line. Elsewhere the straits are in general at least ten fathoms deep.

The other area where a lower sea level in antiquity might have altered the terrain is in the area of Ambelaki Bay, which is the southernmost bay, probably held by the Aeginetans. The effect of this would be to reduce the area of this bay. However the *general* sea level cannot have been shallower in antiquity, as otherwise the southern harbour of Piraeus (Zea) would have been dry land, and unsuitable for the main classical Athenian naval base which it was! Its modern depth is about a fathom.

The straits themselves are on average 2,000 yds. wide approximately, and follow a winding course past the Greek anchorages. The entrance to the straits is closed by the long spit of the Cynosura (Dog's Tail) peninsula,

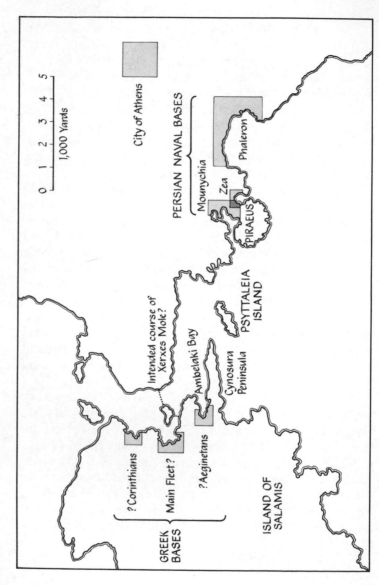

Fig. 18. Salamis – the eastern straits and surrounding area.

and by the island of Psyttaleia, which is in the middle of the entrance to the straits. It is the entrance to the straits which is of most interest. On either side of the island of Psyttaleia the strait is only about 1,000 yds. wide, and an enemy coming through past Psyttaleia is therefore restricted to a split frontage of 2,000 yds.

But a fleet waiting on the north side of Psyttaleia can form an L shaped line 3,000 yds. long, so that the two columns coming through the passages either side of Psyttaleia face an enemy with 50 per cent more ships in action (if both are using the same interval between ships).

This is the one place in the Salamis straits where the defender has that kind of advantage; elsewhere the fleets would meet on an equal frontage. Therefore the Greek fleet would have secure flanks if it fought anywhere within the Salamis strait; if it fought immediately north of Psyttaleia island, it would actually fight with secure flanks *and* have an advantage of frontage over the enemy.

But this particular position has one further deadly characteristic. Suppose that an enemy passes through and is allowed to form line north of Psyttaleia. In the event of any reverse, then the retreating fleet would be forced into two bottlenecks, and thrown into confusion.

There is a further peculiarity of the terrain which is worth mentioning, and this is a weather situation which occurs from time to time, and can be predicted by seamen familiar with the locality. A southerly wind creates a swell in the Saronic Gulf, which comes up into the straits, and makes choppy water within them.

These peculiarities of the terrain were the basis of the deadly deception and trap which the Greek commanders had prepared for the Persians.

An integral part of this plan was the number of ships available. The Persians originally had about 800 ships, now reduced by losses in the storm and the battles off Artemisium to perhaps 450. Of the four fleets postulated, that of Cyprus had probably had most battle casualties at Artemisium (30 ships being lost in the first day's fighting in which a Cypriot prince was captured, and a number of Cilician ships being mauled in the second day's action) and it is possible that this fleet had been broken up and used to reinforce the other three, each perhaps now about 150 strong. More plausibly, the fleet of Cyprus was used to reinforce the fleets of Phoenicia and Ionia, bringing their total strength to about 350 effectives, with the fleet of Egypt (commanded by Satrap of Egypt, and forming a single identifiable unit) being undiluted at about 100 strong. With a 50 yd. interval between ships, even in three lines the Persian fleet would require a frontage of some 7,500 yds., far more than could be accommodated in the Salamis strait.

The Greek fleet was, despite the reinforcements from Pogon, smaller than at Artemisium, and with a 20 per cent loss there, plus the reinforcements which it had received, was now slightly over 300 strong.

8
The Battle

◆◇◆◇◆◇◆

The Greek Deception

The first of the incidents of the battle itself, and the trigger of the action, was started by Themistocles, the Athenian commander, evidently with the knowledge and approval of his colleagues. He selected a trustworthy agent, Sicinnus, who was one of his own household slaves, and in charge of his children. Sicinnus took a boat and crossed to the Persian fleet, and delivered the following message to the admirals.

Sicinnus stated that Themistocles had sent him without the knowledge of the other Greek commanders, and that Themistocles was really a supporter of the Persians. As proof of this, Themistocles was passing on information that the Greeks were disunited and could not agree on a common policy. The opportunity was therefore there for a great Persian success, and Sicinnus concluded "you will see them fighting among themselves, your supporters and those against you."

Such is the message as recounted by Herodotus. Aeschylus in his play *The Persians* gives a substantially similar account, but confines the message to saying that the Greeks were abandoning the Salamis position, and after dark would break out, each contingent going its own way. He does not mention Themistocles by name, partly because of the requirements of the verse, partly because Themistocles was the opposition, politically, as far as the hoplite and aristocratic classes, to which Aeschylus belonged, were concerned.

Modern scholars have sometimes doubted the story as given by Aeschylus and Herodotus, but deliberately feeding false information to an enemy is a well-known means of deception, and the story is first recorded by a combatant (Aeschylus) within eight years of the battle.

The genuineness of the message must, for different reasons, have been the subject of equally keen debate by the Persian command. At first sight it represented a first class piece of intelligence of the utmost importance. Was it a plant? Why should the commander of the Athenian contingent, when the Athenians were known to be the most implacable enemies of Persia, send such a message?

The very audacity of Themistocles' bluff in fact ensured that the message would be accepted. Themistocles was a politician of immense skill and experience, and he had successfully read the minds of his opponents. The message he sent them was exactly what they wanted to hear, and exactly confirmed what the 'experts' in the Persian camp must have been saying about the Greeks for weeks: The Greeks cannot combine, they will fall out, the alliance will split. The very fact that Themistocles sent the message will have been confirmation in the cynical minds of men who were used to buying their way where they could not get by force of arms. Even the most implacable enemy of Persia, they will have said, tries to ingratiate himself when all is lost.

The Persians, then, accepted the message as genuine, and acted upon it. The night following the message from Sicinnus, they made their dispositions to meet the anticipated break-out by the Greeks. Again we must look at what our sources say they intended to do.

Herodotus states that they landed troops on the island of Psyttaleia, in the anticipation that men and crippled ships would be washed ashore here in the course of the battle, and the troops on the island would be able to assist their friends.

The Persian ships were disposed by night, with the west wing towards Salamis for encirclement, and a cordon on the strait as far as Munychia.

Aeschylus states that the Persians ordered their ships to move by night in three lines (or bodies?) to close off the exits from the Salamis strait.

The Persian intention so far is clear. Faced with an expected Greek break-out, they intended to prevent the escape of their foes, and to destroy them at a disadvantage. What in detail were their dispositions?

There are two exits from the Greek position, one to the east of Salamis, with the island of Psyttaleia sitting squarely in the middle, one to the west. There was evidently from Herodotus' account a cordon from the coast of Salamis to Munychia, a distance of perhaps 7,000 yds., if the cordon was about 1,000 yds. south of Psyttaleia. This distance could be covered by a frontage of 140 ships, if ships were at an interval of 50 yds.

The second exit from the Salamis strait is through the western channel, which is narrow and twisting, and in places only 600 yds. wide. Some ships might be expected to break out here – it would be the shortest route back to Corinth, for instance, but provided the Greeks were not expecting the Persians to be waiting, which is what the Persians believed, then the majority would be coming through the eastern exit, the Athenians even perhaps to Xerxes' camp to make their submission. A force would therefore have to watch the western exit, but the main effort would be at the eastern.

If the Persians had effectively three fleets left, the dispositions suggested themselves. The Egyptian fleet, possibly now 100 strong, was to seal the western exit, the Phoenician and Ionian fleets, with the remnants of the conglomerate 'fleet of Cyprus' were to block up the eastern straits. If the fleets off the eastern straits were to form line three deep and had about 350 ships, they could cover the 7,000 yd. gap very conveniently, with a somewhat open formation and plenty of room for manoeuvre.

The Persian fleet movement was made after nightfall, so that it would not be detected by the Greeks. The question is, how long was it supposed to remain secret? If, as is probable, the battle took place about 20th September, the moon rose somewhat before midnight.

Herodotus states that the Persians began their move about the middle of the night. The operation which they planned was a complex one, to be carried out without lights, and moonlight would be essential to ensure that the ships actually took position where they were supposed to. They could be sure that for the same navigational reasons the Greeks would not start their own movement before moonrise. If both fleets started at moonrise the Persians would have time to get into position before the Greeks could escape.

There was a further pressing reason why the Persians needed the light of the moon to assist their cordons maintain station – the depth of water where they proposed to set their cordons is over 30 fathoms, making anchoring difficult, and ensuring that the ships had to be rowed up and down for hours. 'Rank hailed rank' hymns Aeschylus, and one can imagine the seamen shouting to each other to avoid collision.

Since the moon had risen, it would be impossible for the Persians to keep the fact that their fleet was at sea secret – but what was the point of secrecy now? Once the ships were in position to foil a Greek break-out, it was merely a matter of finishing off the disorganised remains in due course. The Persians could hardly be expecting to fight a night battle against Greek forces trying to break out, but if they did, then the moonlight would give them light to see, and the open water sufficient room for their favourite tactics.

No, the Persians believed that the Greek fleet had collapsed through internal disunity, and would be easy prey.

In fact the Persians were playing right into the hands of Themistocles and the Greeks. By inducing the Persians to put to sea in the middle of the night and cordon off the exits, Themistocles had ensured that by the time dawn came and the Persians entered the straits, they would have had their rowers at the oars for at least six hours, and they would be fatigued in consequence. Even in open water, let alone the confined waters of the straits, a fresh Greek crew might now have the edge over them.

How likely is it that the Persians might have attempted to enter the straits by night? Themistocles must have been confident that they would not. Their aim was not to fight before dawn, merely to contain the Greek fleet, and a movement into the straits might have precipitated action against Greek vessels.

The deception plan which Themistocles had devised thus ensured: first: that the Persians would enter the straits at dawn; second: that they would do so with tired crews; and third: that they would meet an enemy with fresh crews in waters ideally suited to his tactics.

Themistocles had also ensured that the Persian fleet entered battle with orders issued the evening before. Even if the Persians on land observing the Greek positions thought that the message was false, they could not convey it to the fleet.

The account of the night moves in Herodotus is full of rather improbable details, as far as the Greek camp is concerned. In the middle of the night he has the Greek command still arguing about the propriety of withdrawing to the Isthmus – no doubt the admirals were in anxious conference, but drawing up their final plans for the morrow's battle. He then introduces the character of Aristides.

Now Aristides (styled, and possibly self-styled, The Just) was a political opponent of Themistocles –

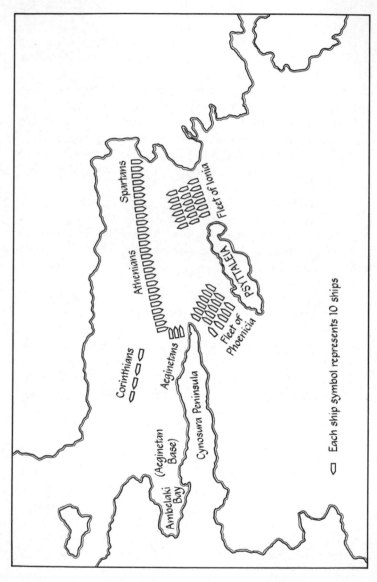

Fig. 19. The deployment of the fleets at the Battle of Salamis.

Spartans

Athenians

Corinthians

Aeginetans

(Aeginetan Base)

Ambelaki Bay

Cynosura Peninsula

Fleet of Ionia

PSYTTALEIA

Fleet of Phoenicia

◁ Each ship symbol represents 10 ships

he commanded the Athenian army in the campaign in the next year, when Themistocles was in eclipse – and his appearance in the story has been explained as an attempt by his supporters to gain some of the credit of Salamis for him, as well as the credit for the battle of Plataea. At any rate, he is said to have passed through the blockade, and come to the Greek camp. Here he called Themistocles out of the conference of the admirals to advise him of what the Persians were doing. Themistocles then asked Aristides to tell his tale to the admirals, most of whom did not believe it, and it was only the arrival of further confirmation in the form of deserters from the Persians which convinced the Greek admirals.

The best that can be said for this story is that it does not say much for the Greek sentinels, who must have been able to watch the Persian moves by moonlight from Salamis.

Whether true or not, at dawn the Greeks were united with a common plan, and ready to move.

At dawn the Persians began to move forward to enter the straits. Some have suggested they must long now have suspected that the message from Themistocles was a trick. This is not necessarily the case for the reasons stated.

Although they had only a short way to move to enter the straits, the movement will have created problems for the Persians. The Phoenicians were on the left, the Ionian fleet on the right, both probably on a 3,500 yd. frontage. In advancing, they had to pass through a strait about 1,000 yds broad, involving for the Phoenicians a change of course as well. They would tend to debouch either side of Psyttaleia in two columns, each about 1,000 yds. frontage.

Meanwhile the Greeks had themselves moved at dawn. At first light the crews were assembled, and given a harangue by their respective contingent commanders. They then embarked and set off, and were rapidly in action.

The deployment of the Greek fleet is critical, and the

differing accounts must be reconciled if we are to make sense of the battle. Herodotus says that the Greeks set out in full force, and they were immediately charged by the Persians. The Greeks began to back water, some until they were on the point of running aground, until one or two ships rammed enemies and so precipitated a general attack on the enemy fleet. The Phoenicians are said to have had the western wing 'nearest Eleusis', the Ionians the eastern, 'nearest Piraeus', and opposing them the Athenians and Spartans respectively.

Aeschylus narrates the battle from the Persian point of view (his account is a speech given by a messenger supposed to have fought in the battle). In his version the Persians first heard the Greeks singing the war chant, the *Paian*, there was a trumpet signal, then the whole Greek fleet suddenly burst into view, in perfect order, with the right wing leading, and the rest of the fleet following. Again in Aeschylus the battle is said to have begun 'immediately', with an Athenian vessel ramming a Phoenician ship. This confirms one of the variants given by Herodotus; the other gives credit to an Aeginetan vessel for the first blow.

The most natural interpretation of Herodotus' account is that the Persians were at this time within the strait, somehow facing south, with their backs to the north shore. The Greeks will then have deployed by coming down the straits on the south side, right wing leading (to bring in the detail recorded by Aeschylus), turned individually to port and were facing the Persians. This puts the Spartans on the right wing (the place of honour, where the C-in-C would be expected to be found), and the Athenians on the left wing, where as second senior contingent (by virtue of numbers) they might be expected to be found.

There are many difficulties to this interpretation, not least being why, even if the Persians deployed in a long line facing south, the Greeks should array themselves opposite, on a long front, instead of attacking the Persian right wing with all their strength and ignoring the rest of the enemy unless they chose to join in. Certainly two of Aeschylus' details cannot be right, because the Persians will have been able to see any Greek ships coming out of Ambelaki bay all the time after they passed north of the line of Cynosura, and it must have taken a considerable time for the Greeks to file down the strait, keeping to their own side.

Early commentators got over this problem by locating the Greek fleet along the north side of the Cynosura promontory, which is extremely rocky!

Most modern accounts place the action close to the Greek beaches, with the Phoenician ships north of the intended site of the mole, and the Ionians behind, both facing approximately southwest. The objection again is, why should the Persians keep respectfully to one side of the strait, ignoring Ambelaki bay, and the Greek ships in it? More seriously, how could they have got so far up the straits in the time available?

The critical factor is how far both sides could have got in the time available to them. The Greeks must have set out from their beaches half-an-hour or so after first light, assembling at first light and embarking after hearing a speech from their commander, including battle orders.

The Persians were at dawn still on their patrol lines, and no doubt it was somewhat after dawn when they finally determined that there was no break-out by the Greeks, and that they would therefore need to enter the straits. With the Greeks setting out somewhat before the Persians, trial deployments on the wargames table showed that they could form a line north of Psyttaleia island, facing south, just before the Persian fleet could enter the straits to engage them.

A further interesting point emerged from trial deployments on the wargames table, confirming Aeschylus' detail that the right wing of the Greek fleet led the way. Most commentators make the Aeginetan contingent the right wing, based on its position in Ambelaki bay (assumed) in the Greek fleet, viewed by an observer looking east. However, one would expect that if the

Greeks did deploy north of Psyttaleia facing south, the left wing would have been in the lead. Some explain this by saying that it was the right wing as the Persians saw it, i.e. the Greek left that led. But a simpler possibility suggested itself from the trial deployments. The force from Ambelaki bay is the first to arrive in the vicinity of a Persian force. Rather than cross the front of that force, exposing itself to being taken in flank, it seemed more logical for those ships to form a short line facing east, with the right wing resting on the Cynosura promontory. The presence of this force makes the Persians check before advancing further northwards, to avoid being taken in flank.

It is thus suggested that the remainder of the Greek fleet, the majority of which was the Athenian contingent, based on the main beaches, was at this time passing to the north of this short Aeginetan line, prior to forming the main line facing south. This deployment will have been led by the Commander-in-Chief, the Spartan Eurybiadas, who will thus have found himself on the extreme left of the Greek line, facing the Ionians; where Herodotus says he was, in fact.

The reference to 'backing water' remains to be explained. The time schedule was tight. It appears likely that the backing water was to enable the Greeks to dress their line, and give themselves a short space of time more before the Persians could attack them.

There is one further, and important result of the Greek fleets backing water. It would suggest to the Persian command that they were reluctant to engage, confirming the false intelligence which had been fed to them by Sicinnus, and encouraging them to press on confidently into the strait.

This point is a convenient one to consider the action of the Corinthian contingent. Herodotus says: 'The Athenians say that Adeimantus, the Corinthian commander, at the very start of the battle, when the ships were engaging, was struck with terror and panic, and hoisted sail and fled, and the rest of the Corinthians

Plate 1 Central Greece as seen by the U.S. Eros satellite, showing the area of the campaign (cf. Fig. 14). The Thermopylae and Artemisium positions appear clearly (left centre), and the advantage of the Greek fleet holding Artemisium is obvious. Not only are the Artemisium beaches the only good ones in the area, but the Persian army is separated from its fleet and supplies by some extremely inhospitable country.

The Salamis area can only dimly be glimpsed through the cloud (bottom right of picture) coming off the Cithaeron/Parnes mountain line, but the Bay of Marathon and the site of the Battle of Plataea show clearly to east and north respectively of this cloud. (A NASA photograph reproduced by courtesy of the U.S. Geological Survey, EROS Data Center)

Plate 2 *A Phoenician trireme modelled to 1/72 scale by the author. Marines are shown (Minifigs Persians and Airfix Syrian archers) but rowers and crew are omitted*

Plate 3 *The wargame in progress: the Persian fleet (right) enters the straits. The L-shaped Greek line (on left) awaits them and the Corinthians make off under sail in the foreground. The Phoenician fleet (nearer camera) can be seen to be in some confusion already.*

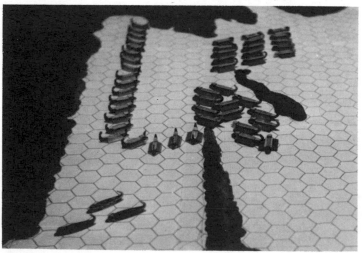

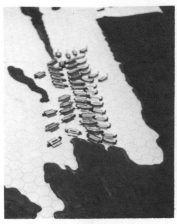

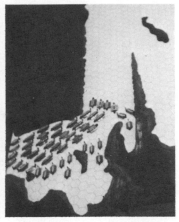

Plate 4 The wargame in pro-
gress : the fleets engage

Plate 5 Wargaming the battle on
the assumption it was fought off
the Greek beaches. The Persian
fleet is nearly enveloped before the
battle starts

Plate 6 Wargaming what the Persians expected but did not get : an
attempted Greek breakout. The Phoenician (bottom left) and Ionian
(bottom right) fleets have plenty of open water for envelopment tactics.
This photograph shows the general layout of the wargame table, with
Psyttaleia in the centre and the straits leading off top left

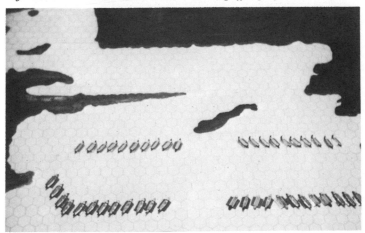

Plate 7   Ancient Greek rock carving of the stern of a classical ship, from Lindos (Rhodes). The ship is a cataphract vessel and therefore later in date than Salamis, but the general shape of the stern will be similar. The port steering oar may be seen swung up above the waterline – the usual practice when beaching a ship, to avoid damage. The author's wife gives an indication of scale – the carving is probably half life-size

seeing him flee, themselves turned and fled.' He goes on to say that they fled a considerable distance, when they were met by some mysterious people in a boat, who told them the battle was won after all, when they turned back, arriving after everything was over. He then goes on to say that no one but the Athenians believes this version, and that the Corinthians were in fact in the forefront of the battle.

There is confirmation of this in the survival of the epitaph of the Corinthians who fell at Salamis, confirming that there were in fact casualties in their contingent.

So obviously the Athenian story is a grossly one-sided version of an incident which actually took place in the battle. What were the orders given to the Corinthians?

The key to the matter is the third Persian fleet, the Egyptians, watching the western exit. A battle fought immediately north of Psyttaleia was a considerable distance from the western exits which the Egyptians were watching, but the possibility had to be faced that the Egyptians would enter the western straits and come round through the bay of Eleusis to fall on the Greek rear. The Corinthians were obviously ordered to move north to guard against this threat. The Greek land forces on the island of Salamis will have been more than sufficient to set up a comprehensive watch and signalling system, and when the Egyptians were seen to be making no attempt to enter the straits this was signalled to a party who set off in a small boat to advise the Corinthians that they need not continue towards the west, but could reinforce the main eastern battle, where all appeared to be going well.

And the circumstances of the Corinthian departure from the main action will have been a further touch of verisimilitude to the Greek deception plan. For hoisting sail was a universal signal that the ships doing so were not going to engage, but were seeking to disengage and escape. Fourteen years before Salamis, the battle of Lade had been the decisive sea battle which destroyed the Ionian rebels against Persian rule, and that battle had started with the Samian contingent abandoning their position, hoisting sail, and running for home. It has been remarked that the captains of the Phoenician fleet must have included men who saw that happen at Lade, and the Ionian fleet may even have included Samians who were in the fleeing ships. It must have seemed to the Persians that the Greeks were indeed disunited and an easy prey.

To summarise, then, how matters appeared to the Persians as they came north past Psyttaleia island. On their left was a small unit (the Aeginetan contingent), in good order, threatening their left flank. Before them was the main Greek fleet, apparently in some disarray, and backing water. At the corner of the L-shaped line which the Greeks were forming, a large contingent (the Corinthians) were hoisting sail and attempting to flee. Evidently the message they had received was true! (This is the situation shown in Fig. 19.)

But in what order was the Persian fleet, and what was the formation they had adopted to pass through the strait either side of Psyttaleia? It has already been stated that a minimum interval between ships in line was likely to be 50 yds. Closer intervals could of course, be maintained, but with one ship every 50 yds. there was just room for every ship to turn if necessary, the absolute minimum degree of manoeuvrability required. By using the oars, one bank forwards, one backwards, a trireme could be pivoted through as many degrees as necessary, and with a length of slightly over 100 ft. would need 60 ft. clear either side of the centre line to pivot through 180°.

Now the Persian fleet had been on a frontage of 7,000 yds. at dawn, and each fleet had to reduce frontage from 3,500 yds. to about 1,000 to pass into the straits. It is worth considering in detail how this was done.

Each ship on a 50 yd. frontage will have physically

Fig. 20. This is the only disciplined way in which the Persians could have reduced their front to enter the straits. Note that considerable open water to front is required for this movement.

MOVEMENT FROM LINE TO COLUMN

1. Ships in 6 columns of 3 vessels

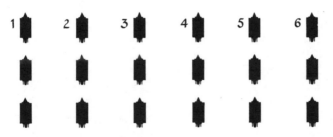

2. Ships in 2 columns of 9 vessels

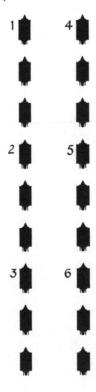

occupied only a quarter or so of the frontage allocated to it, so it would in theory have been possible for the columns merely to have sailed very close to each other (each column three ships deep) to contract the frontage to the necessary degree. This would have resulted in the ships sailing so close together that collisions would be inevitable.

Thus, merely reducing frontage without increasing depth by packing more ships into a given area of sea was not the answer. It was necessary for the Persians to increase the depth of the files of ships in their formation. In contemporary land warfare this was done by one file dropping behind another, and no doubt a similar system was adopted here. If the files were increased from 3 ships deep to 12 ships deep, the frontage would in theory be reduced to just under 900 yds, while the depth of the formation was increased to 850 from about 250 yds. This is how it could be done in theory.

But how was it done in practice, by a fleet consisting of many contingents from different areas, all with different standards of skill and training? The larger, better-trained contingents will have carried out a satisfactory manoeuvre. But the smaller units – and a number of smaller units will have contained less than 12 ships – will have carried out their own versions. It must also be borne in mind that each ship had a Persian marine contingent on board, no doubt totally ignorant of naval manoeuvres, but alert for any signs of shirking or dereliction of duty.

We may therefore assume that the Persian fleet passed the island of Psyttaleia in two compact bodies or columns, but that there had been both straggling and bunching, so that in many places the interval between ships was less than was desirable, while some other ships had fallen slightly back.

On passing north of the island and reaching relatively open water, the Persians must have attempted to extend their columns, to restore a line formation and so match the Greek frontage. In theory the leading ships should

Fig. 21. Forming line again from column. This is the manoeuvre the Persians had to execute in face of the Greek fleet. Note that columns 4 and 6 have been transposed. The more ships there are in the column trying to extend, the more complicated and open to confusion the manoeuvre. The Persians were trying to carry it out with columns probably 16 or 17 ships across and 9 deep!

have diverged so that the ships behind them could come up and create the former number of files. But to do this in the face of the enemy meant that the ships would have to expose their broadsides, at least partially, while the front was being extended. For obvious reasons some captains will have been reluctant to do so; others will automatically have halted on seeing the enemy deployed in front of them.

The result was that the columns, in deploying, became further disorganised. And at this point the Greeks attacked the enemy, at least some of whose vessels were also pressing forward to attack the Greeks.

The action now became general, both Herodotus and Aeschylus stressing that the Greeks were fighting in an ordered and disciplined formation, while the Persian fleet was disorganised and in confusion. If the wind from the south, which is mentioned by Plutarch (and it was favourable to the Corinthians), was blowing, it will have aided the confusion, since the high sterns and sides of the Phoenician vessels will have tended to catch the wind, broaching the ship to, and turning it broadside on to the Greeks. The major factor in the disarray of the Persians was, however, the lack of space for deployment. According to Aeschylus, collisions were even taking place between ships of the Persian fleet.

The Greeks had succeeded in getting a fleet action entirely on their own terms. The Persians were in narrow waters where they had no space for their skilled tactics, and no way of finding an open flank to get behind the Greeks. The only way to victory was straight ahead, by overcoming the Greek marines – and the troops who had shown themselves best able to deal with hoplites, the Egyptians, were elsewhere. In fact, so far were the Persians from finding a Greek flank that they themselves were fighting on two fronts, with the Aeginetans attacking the left end of the Phoenician fleet. The Greek commanders had reason to be content: they had got their ships into a position which gave their crews every chance to destroy the enemy.

The boarding battle which now ensued made the result of the battle of Salamis certain. While a number of Phoenician and Ionian ships could not avoid being rammed and sunk in the press of vessels, the majority were carried by boarding. But it should not be assumed that the Persians did not resist strongly. They fought well, according to Herodotus, much better than off Artemisium; and indeed at Salamis their efforts were being watched by Xerxes in person from a convenient point on the mountainside overlooking the straits.

Persian resistance, indeed, is said to have continued for most of the day, and a number of individual captains had successes over their Greek opponents. In a congested battle such as Salamis, the pace must indeed have been slow. A rammed ship would sink, but not entirely; it would float waterlogged. Ships, once taken, equally could not be sent to the rear because there was not effective space to move them. After most of the Persian front rank had become casualties, they would thus tend to create a wall of ships through which neither side could readily pass, and the battle must have settled down into a series of individual fights with no grand movements of squadrons, but each captain doing his best to get within striking distance of an enemy vessel.

RESULT OF LEAVING INSUFFICIENT SPACE BETWEEN SHIPS

Difficulty of turning with only 35 yards between ships' axes

0   20   40   60   80   100 Scale in yards

Fig. 22. This is the problem the Persians faced if their front contracted to an excessive degree. Insufficient space is left for ships to turn and retire in order to retreat.

Eventually the point was reached when the Persians had had enough, and turned to fly. Even this presented problems, as a ship wishing to escape had to turn through 180°, requiring a pivot on its axis, and necessitating a circle of clear water 120 ft. across at least. During this movement, the turning ship would be extremely vulnerable and no doubt many Persian vessels were sunk or disabled in turning, or fell foul of their own side. But turn they did, and the survivors of the fleet headed back as fast as possible to the passages either side of Cynosura. The Greeks pursued, and it is in this stage of the battle, with some at least of the combatants finding relatively open water, that the vivid incidents retailed by Herodotus belong. Artemisia, Queen of Halicarnassus, fought on the Persian side, and gets a disproportionate amount of coverage as Halicarnassus was Herodotus' own birthplace. In the pursuit she was being overhauled by an Athenian – she rammed one of her own allies and the Athenian seeing the incident mistook her for a friend and sheered off. Xerxes, sitting on his lofty seat, also observed the incident, and took favourable note of Artemisia's zeal and fighting spirit, thinking she had rammed a Greek ship!

The Aeginetans merit special mention at this stage of the battle. In their position on the flank of the Phoenician fleet, they were well placed to cause casualties to the fleeing enemy.

At last the survivors of the Persian fleet won south past Psyttaleia, and returned to Phaleron. They must have been desperately tired, since most of them had been at their oars for nearly 24 hours. Despite their relative freshness, the Greeks did not press the pursuit, but secured the wrecks and prizes, and returned to their anchorages.

Only one further action took place on the day. The Persian garrison on Psyttaleia had watched the course of the battle, and were now isolated. The Greek forces (Athenians mostly) on Salamis had equally been frustrated of action; but now they sent a landing party across to the island, took it, and killed the garrison.

What were the results of Salamis, in terms of casualties? The sources give few details. One late source gives the Greek loss at 40 ships, the Persian at 200, which is possible. If so, the Greek fleet would have been reduced to about 270 vessels, of which some would be requiring various degrees of repair. The Persians, however, would have been down to 250, and in no condition to re-engage. One factor noted was that the Greeks who lost their ships could save themselves by swimming back to Salamis (or another nearby ship), while the Persians could not, and drowned. If such were indeed the case, then the ability of the Greeks to bring damaged vessels or prizes into action later in the campaign if necessary will not have been hampered by lack of crews to the same extent as the Persians.

If the fighting took a similar course to that off Artemisium, and casualties were in a similar proportion, then we may suggest the following figures for losses in the battle of Salamis.

Persian Fleet :	Initial strength	Losses	Strength after Salamis
Fleet of Phoenicia			
Fleet of Ionia	350	200	150
Fleet of Cyprus (rump)			
Fleet of Egypt	100	–	100

Greek Fleet :			
Initial strength	Total losses	Cripples	Persian prizes
310	40	60	120

Total strength immediately after battle –   210 ships
Potential strength with cripples and prizes – 390 ships

It will be noted that it has been assumed that in both cases the reported losses (200 and 40 for Persians and Greeks respectively) are the final losses. Salamis was a hard-fought battle which went on for a considerable time, and while the Greeks had a killing time when the Persians turned to flee, a casualty ratio of 5 : 1 is high. However, if we accept the same proportion of damaged to total losses as appears to have been the case at Artemisium, then we get the battle casualties as 100 for the Greeks and 200 for the Persians, giving a ratio of 2 : 1. The difference was that since the Greeks ended the day in possession of the straits, they could recover all their own crippled vessels and the Persian prizes, and their long term position was, therefore, much better.

9
Results
of the Battle

◆◆◆◆◆◆◆

As with many battles, the victors did not immediately
realise that they had won an overwhelming triumph.
The Greeks secured the cripples and wrecks as far as
they could, although the westerly wind which blew up
towards the end of the battle washed many of the wrecks
up on the coast east of Phaleron, suggesting that some of
the ships at least must have continued the pursuit past
the island of Psyttaleia. Their own fleet was restored to
the best order possible, and they expected that the
Persians would again make an attack upon them.

It was only after a period that they realised that though
the Persian army was maintaining its position, the fleet
had gone. Although an immediate pursuit was ordered,
it was too late to come up to the escaping enemy, who
made their way across the Aegean. The Greek fleet
accordingly came to the island of Andros, and there
debated what to do next.

Their present position was an obvious one, controlling
the route which any supply vessel trying to reinforce the
Persians would have to use, and covering the entrance to

the Saronic Gulf, so that any Persian fleet could not return without risking a battle.

There were two strategic options open to the Greeks, which may be called 'offensive' and 'defensive'.

The offensive option was that proposed by Themistocles, who was in favour of exploiting the strategic initiative gained by the battle of Salamis to cut the line of retreat of the Persian army, and rely on winter and lack of supplies to destroy it utterly. To accomplish this he proposed that the Greek fleet should at once set out for the Hellespont, which they could occupy without any difficulty, and there break down the pontoon bridges (which in fact were carried away by a storm about this time, forcing the Persians to cross by ship – presumably the ships which had formed the pontoons). A Greek fleet occupying the east bank of the Hellespont could keep Xerxes and the survivors of his army on the west side indefinitely.

It was a characteristic of Spartan tactics that they never pursued a defeated enemy with vigour, a perhaps arrogant attitude brought about by their certainty that if he attacked again he would be driven off again. So it was the Spartans and their allies who opposed the strategy of Themistocles with one of their own. The Spartan view was that the Persians' position was now untenable and that they would retreat in any case. Under the circumstances a further invasion was not likely. The interests of the Greeks would thus not be served by seeking to *prevent* Xerxes' retreat. The crux of the Spartan position was that the Persians were basically a vigorous and energetic people, and Xerxes a ruler of ability. If trapped in Greece or in Thrace he could be expected to act ruthlessly to retain as large a force as he could, and no one could tell what he might not succeed in doing, once pressed to it.

Negative as these tactics might be, such was the policy adopted by the Greeks, and no offensive move was made, apart from expeditions to collect indemnities from islands in the Aegean and coastal cities which had supported the Persians.

It is at this point that Herodotus makes Themistocles send a further message to Xerxes, suggesting that the Greeks were planning to attack the Hellespont, and that he had better retreat to secure his escape. It is suspicious that one of the reported messengers was Sicinnus, whose cover was now presumably thoroughly 'blown', and it may be asked why the Persians needed Themistocles to point out obvious strategic dangers to them.

The possibility of re-engaging by sea must have been considered by the Persians after Salamis, but rejected. Probably crucial was the attitude of the Phoenicians, who are reported to have gone home immediately after the battle, and were certainly not at Mycale the following year when the final battle of the war was fought at sea. No doubt the first reaction of the Phoenician commanders was that they had been forced to give battle in totally unfavourable circumstances through the ineptitude of their Persian overlords, and there must have been hints of mutiny at any suggestion of re-engaging. If the Phoenicians had been forced to mutiny by the Persians seeking another battle, the consequences for Xerxes would have been disastrous. He might hope to withdraw the greater part of his army by prompt action back to Persian territory, but his position would be immeasurably complicated if in the meantime dissident subject contingents had returned home and were raising revolt with impunity. Egypt had revolted within the past 10 years. If Phoenicia now revolted, the consequences would be incalculable.

The fleet was accordingly permitted to retire at once, and the Persians gave up all hope of re-engaging by sea. The question was, what was to be done with the land army?

The main problem was that of supplying the soldiers; with the fleet defeated there was no protection for the ships, as the Greeks could outflank the Persians with their fleet with impunity. This was in fact a peculiarity of the Aegean, with its many islands, forming potential bases for ships. When Alexander invaded Persia 150 years later, he neutralised the Persian fleet with land forces simply by occupying the coastline of Asia Minor, and depriving it of landing and watering places. This was not possible for the Persians.

The solution which was adopted was to leave behind a large land force, presumably as large as could be supported from local resources, while the remainder of the army, under Xerxes himself, returned to Asia. This move was carried out a few days after Salamis. Mardonius, the Satrap designate of Greece, remained with the best Persian troops, including the Immortals and the Median and Persian infantry proper, forces with which to reopen the campaign in the next year, supported by the Thebans, Thessalians, and other Medizing Greeks.

Xerxes' retreat was endowed in Greek stories with as many hardships and disasters as Napoleon's retreat from Moscow: certainly the Persians requisitioned supplies freely and could have been in serious difficulties feeding even that part of the army with Xerxes (probably about two thirds or three quarters of the total). However, the retreat was in fact accomplished in good order, and provision was, for instance, made for the care of the sick at various stages along the route. The immediate results of the battle were thus the complete defeat of the Persian invasion of Greece, and the withdrawal of most of the invaders to their homeland.

In the following year, the emphasis shifted to land, and the remainder of the Persian army was annihilated at the battle of Plataea when Mardonius attacked the combined free Greek army. He himself was killed, and his Persian troops were annihilated. The only Persian troops to escape were those commanded by a colleague who was tardy to engage, saw how things were with the battle, and turned about and fled to Asia before anyone could intercept him and his troops.

In the meantime the Greek fleet had sought out and destroyed the remainder of the Persian fleet at Mycale on the west coast of Asia Minor. The Persian fleet was now so inferior that it could not even fight at sea, and it was drawn up on the shore and protected by field fortifications. The battle which ensued was thus a land battle as the marines from the Greek fleet landed and stormed the Persian position.

In the years following Salamis, the Greeks retained the initiative against Persia, although the leadership now effectively passed to Athens, leading a confederation of Aegean states which in time became more and more a tributary empire. The Athenian strategy, offensive in character, which had been proposed by Themistocles, was now carried on by his political rivals, and Athenian fleets ranged as far afield as Egypt in following years. Finally, in 449–8 B.C., the Athenian statesman Callias negotiated a settlement with the Persians whereby the Greeks of Asia Minor were confirmed in their freedom, and Persian warships were barred from the Aegean.

The victory of Salamis had more far-reaching effects. The Athenian fleet rose in importance, following the victory, and came to dominate the Aegean. New tactical methods made the Athenians the most skilful naval power in the area, far superior to any other Greek fleet. The Athenian conversion of the Aegean league against Persia into an empire with Athens at the centre gave an impetus to the Athenians which found its flower in Periclean Athens. More remotely, the Persian invasion of Greece was constantly cited as a reason for Greeks to invade Persia, and Alexander the Great eventually used the invasion of Xerxes as his *casus belli* when he crossed the Hellespont 150 years later.

As to the characters who played the most important parts, little is known of their subsequent careers. Xerxes made no further attempts to invade Greece, and was assassinated in a court intrigue about 15 years after Salamis. Most of the Greek commanders lived out their lives held in respect in their cities. Adeimantus, the Corinthian, had a son whom we find fighting against the Athenians 50 years later in the seige of Potidaea.

94

Sicinnus the secret agent was well rewarded: Themistocles made him a wealthy man and obtained for him the citizenship of the city of Histiaea. In fact Themistocles himself was the least well-rewarded of the Greek commanders. In the year following Salamis, the strategic emphasis switched to the land, the command passed to his opponent Aristides, and he failed even to be elected one of the ten Generals. Ten years of political intrigue followed, at the end of which he was exiled from Athens and two years later he was condemned to death in his absence. He accordingly fled by a circuitous route to Persia, where he was honourably received and given the Lordship of three cities by Artaxerxes, the successor to Xerxes. (Two of the cities were in revolt from Persian control, which made the bounty slightly less generous!). It is ironic that the man who did most to ensure that Greece should remain free of Persian control should have ended his days in comfort, as a pensioner of the Persian government.

10
Consequences
of a Persian
Victory

◆◇◆◇◆◇

While, in general, historical speculation is a barren exercise, when wargamers are reconstructing a campaign, they must obviously have some indication of the likely consequences of a Persian victory, either at Artemisium or at Salamis.

Let us suppose – considering Artemisium first – that the storm which had conveniently reduced the odds against the Greeks, did not in fact arise. In this case the Persians would still have had their difficulties in deploying their full forces at Artemisium, but they would have been able to place 200 ships below the narrows of the Euripus, which would have been faced by the 50 Athenian ships placed there. Because of the narrowness of the strait, however, it is unlikely that the Persians would have broken through at that point.

However, after Leonidas was defeated, the Greek fleet retreating down the Euripus would have had to fight its way through this large Persian force. The narrowness of the strait would then have aided the defending Persians, and it is quite possible that the

Greeks in turn would not have been able to break through.

In this event, the Greeks would have been caught between the 200 ships to the south, and the Persian fleet of over 500 ships to the north. As a result they would probably have had to destroy their remaining ships, and retreat by land. Athens was already likely to be evacuated, and we may imagine the Athenian population being withdrawn to the Peloponnese, while the land forces prepared to defend the Isthmus line.

Assuming the campaign to have followed its actual historical course down to the beginning of September, with both sides taking up their positions at Salamis and Phaleron respectively, we can consider a Persian victory likely resulting from a genuine (as distinct from pretended) split in the Greek unity. If this had indeed happened we may imagine the Greek forces abandoning Salamis, and breaking out either by land or sea. In the case of a land breakout, the Greeks would have retired through Megara to the Isthmus, taking the Athenian refugees on Salamis with them. A sea breakout would either have been to Pogon, or more probably, to the Isthmus of Corinth.

In either case, we have a situation in which the Persians would be in a position to advance their land forces to the Isthmus line, supported by their supply ships, and by an overwhelming naval force.

With this in mind, we must next consider the likely actions of the individual Greek cities, faced with the basic alternatives of resistance, surrender, or flight.

The Greeks still resisting would have fallen into three separate classes – the Spartans, the remaining Peloponnesians, and the Athenians and other Greeks resident north of the Isthmus.

The Spartans first. Confident of the Isthmus defences, and discounting any danger from the Persian fleet, they are unlikely to have done anything but fight on. The Peloponnesian allies would probably have followed their example, at this stage.

The Athenians and the others north of the Isthmus, however, are almost certain to have seen things differently. Already unconvinced of the value of fighting on the Isthmus by land with an enemy possessing both land and sea forces, the likelihood is that they would either have surrendered or made their escape.

One must remember that the Athenians had already threatened to quit the alliance and remove their entire population to the west, setting up a colony in Italy or Sicily. If events had taken place as suggested, it is most probable that this is what they would have done, particularly if their fleet remained largely intact. Collecting their refugees and, crossing the Isthmus by the ship portage, they would have set off for the west. Possibly the Megarians and Aeginetans would have followed them, although more probably they would have made their peace with the Persians and accepted terms, no doubt generous ones.

The next stage of the campaign would, logically, have been the assault on the Isthmus line. The Persians should certainly have been able to utilise their superiority in ships at this stage. There are several beaches west of the Isthmus near Corinth on which triremes could land troops, as the Athenians themselves demonstrated 60 years later in the Peloponnesian war. We may therefore quite reasonably envisage Xerxes mounting a land assault on the Greek lines, while the fleet landed Hydarnes and the Immortals behind their flank.

Faced with a repetition of the situation at Themopylae, the Greeks could only have fled or been destroyed, and the northern Peloponnese would have fallen into Persian hands.

This point would have signalled the approaching end of the campaigning season of 480 B.C. Xerxes would therefore have retired to Persia with a solid success achieved, and the fleet could be withdrawn. A large part of the land forces would also have been withdrawn, leaving Mardonius as Satrap of Greece with a strong Persian presence, probably based in Corinth. The winter would have been spent in diplomatic activity, with Mardonius preparing for the subjugation of Sparta in the spring of 479 B.C. It is reasonable to suppose that Argos would have joined the Persians at this stage, if not before, filled with hatred against her traditional enemy, Sparta.

In the spring of 479 B.C., then, the Persians, accompanied by their Greek allies, especially Argos and Boeotia, would have invaded Laconia. With their numbers – possibly 25,000 Persian troops and at least an equal number of Greeks – totalling five times as many as the Spartans could raise, Sparta would have been overwhelmed after a furious resistance.

The results therefore of a Persian victory at Salamis would most probably have been a Satrapy of Greece, under the rule of Mardonius. Meanwhile in the west, the arrival of the numerous and vigorous Athenians would have created a considerable shift in the balance of power. It is not too fanciful to imagine that the Athenians would have succeeded in making themselves the dominant power (instead of Syracuse) in that area in due course, and might well have established themselves as a leading commercial and naval power, as they did in the 5th Century anyway. As such, they would have been rivals of Carthage, and would soon have been involved in conflict with that power, a conflict which they and the other Greeks could have won outright.

In the longer term, defeat at Salamis might thus have meant a new Athens in the west, with Athens holding both Sicily and Carthage. Meanwhile the growing degeneracy of the Persian Empire, and the continual tendency of Satraps to try to make themselves independent, might have left Greece sufficiently weakened for the Athenians to try to reconquer their homeland.

As for Themistocles, so wily a statesman would probably have been long before this a trusted counsellor of the King of Kings; disgraced at Athens following the failure of his naval strategy, his plausible tongue would surely have ensured him a welcome in the Persian camp!

11

Transferring
the Battle to the
Wargames' Table
◆◆◆◆◆◆◆◆◆◆

The problem of simulating Salamis as a wargame is that of reducing action which was spread at its largest extent over an area of at least 25 square miles (on the assumption that only the day of the battle is simulated), and involving 750 ships and 150,000 men, to an area of some 25 square feet, involving only a few players. If the entire campaign is fought as a strategic game, there may well not be a battle of Salamis at all. If the Greeks try to hold Tempe, then they are likely to be destroyed without a naval battle. If they fight in the Thermopylae Artemisium position, it is to be expected that they will hold that line, unless the land battle goes against them, and the Persians will eventually have to retreat into Thessaly. In this case there will also be no battle of Salamis!

Equally, if the Greek decision is not to fight at Salamis, but fall back on the Isthmus, then there is likely to be a disastrous defeat for the Greeks in waters where they cannot hope to protect their flanks.

Leaving aside the strategic problems for the moment,

let us confine ourselves to the problem of fighting the action which took place on the night and day of Salamis, in the actual Salamis straits. The aim of the simulation is to create a wargame which can take place on a reasonably-sized table, and will take not more than about 4 hours to play. This is governed by the practical consideration of the amount of facilities which a wargamer is likely to be able to command, and such external factors as how long his family is likely to be prepared to go without another meal! In addition, the operation must be capable of being controlled by two people (or one if the wargamer prefers to fight solo). In a large wargame meeting it is often interesting to set up a long game with several participants, but such games cannot normally be reproduced every day.

It is a further criterion that the wargame should not involve large quantities of expensive apparatus, and most important, that the action should be covered by mutually agreed, and comprehensive, rules.

The rules themselves are especially crucial, and the next chapter will be devoted to a discussion of the particular rules to be adopted, and the problems which have to be overcome in the simulation of Salamis. In general, however, the criteria which determine whether rules are good or not may be briefly touched upon. The rules should be simple and clear, yet should be comprehensive enough to cover any tactical option which either player may wish to adopt. Paramount is the need for the rules to give a good game. The weighting which the drafter of the rules gives to the factors governing ancient naval operations is thus critical.

Let us therefore now turn to the various factors involved.

The first problem is that of ground scale. A realistic game must try to represent the battle to scale with the original – but to include the Greek and Persian-occupied beaches, the eastern and western straits round Salamis, and the island itself, is to represent an area of about 30,000 yds. from east to west, and 15–20,000 yds. deep.

If the maximum dimension on the wargames table is to be no more than about 8 ft., which is as much as is normally obtainable, then 1 ft. on the table will represent a distance of 4,000 yds. On this basis, a single ship, being 40 yds. long, will be one hundredth of a foot long or about ⅛th of one inch; in metric terms 3 mm. To fight a wargame with ships of this size you would need a magnifying glass and tweezers, which is not a practical possibility . . .

However, suppose that any necessary strategic moves are to be dealt with on an appropriate map of suitable scale, with only any suitable conflict being fought on the table. With a table of say 6 ft. × 4 ft., and ship models of reasonable size – about 1 inch long – you can represent an area of 6,000 × 4,000 ft. This is very close to 1:1200, which is a recognised ship modelling scale, but the battle of Salamis covered a larger area than 6,000 × 4,000 ft., so this scale is not sufficient to recreate the battle.

This problem is still further accentuated if ships of larger scale are to be represented on the table. To take a scale of 1:720 or 1:600, in which individual triremes will be at least 2 inches long, will reduce the area on the table to a quarter of that available at 1:1200. Larger scales will, of course, reduce it still further.

Thus an important restriction has been established, which is that any scale which allows a trireme to be represented in a convenient size for handling will be too large to permit the entire action of the battle of Salamis to be represented on an average table. In other words, if the wargame attempts to represent the battle on a one model equals one ship basis, the action will have to be split, with part of the battle being fought, then the table cleared, and then a further part of the battle being fought. This is likely to be inconvenient, because events in one part of the battle are likely to have an important bearing on those in another part.

This question of scale applies with equal force, or greater, to the question of the men involved in the battle. Wargames on land are now normally fought with troops of 20/25 mm. scale; that is, with figures about one inch high, each of which represents several men. Smaller scales are being increasingly adopted, such as 5 mm., to permit the representation of men on an individual basis.

But even on 5 mm scale, soldiers would be out of scale with the ships, each individual figure being, to scale, 30 ft. tall. Our ancestors were greater than ourselves, so they say, but this is excessive!

No, the representation of individual men in the same action as the ships is not practicable, and because of the scale problem, the men will have to go.

How then are they to be represented? Well, strictly speaking, it is the *effect* of the men which has to be represented. Thus, in the Salamis context, if a Greek ship makes contact with a Persian, it may be expected to board and take it. Provided, therefore, that we can find a reasonable method of representing the effects of men boarding or firing missiles, and covering the different types of soldiers involved, it should not be necessary to represent the marines either individually or as a group with physical figures.

This gives a further benefit from the time point of view. If we attempt to represent on any sort of individual basis the engagements which were fought out in a hundred or more (literally) boarding actions, which is what happened at Salamis, then the time taken will be far more than the average wargamer can be expected to have available. Or be able to endure! A well known writer on battles frequently refers to *lassitudo certaminis*, the weariness which prevents troops at the end of a hard-fought day taking full advantage of a victory. An equal battle fatigue is likely to strike the wargamer if he has to fight a hundred almost identical boarding battles in paralysing detail.

A maximum of four hours has been already mentioned as a convenient length for the wargame. Practical experience shows that 8–10 individual game turns or periods is best for play – continuing time has to be split into a series of individual stages, like a film – and this means that the individual periods will each have to be about 30 minutes long. This is 'playing time', as for the day-long battle each period represents a 'real life time' of over one hour.

In the 30 minutes which is the average period, the wargamer must move all the ships, and must adjudicate the various results of the conflicts which arise in the course of play; and, of course, in the same time span his opponent must be doing the same. Thus there is a physical limit to the amount of individual actions a wargamer can carry out. Basically we can say that if a number of ships have to be handled, rules must be simple and fast in operation, and, if complicated rules are to be adopted, then only a very few ships can be handled. The average time for movement and so forth is only a few seconds, if more than 100 ships are on the table. Thus time, as well as scale, is a further reason why there is a difficulty in representing the full 750 ships at Salamis in one great battle game. However, for each player to control up to 150 ships can be done with suitable rules without any difficulty.

A further problem with timescale has to be dealt with. If each period of the battle represents over an hour's play, how are we to deal with all that can happen within one hour? For instance a ship at 3 knots can traverse a distance of 6,000 yds., and this is going to take it right off the table in one swift movement! In the wargame context the relation of 'actual time' to 'playing time' is THE PROBLEM, and no solution has yet been found which is entirely satisfactory. The only solution, which is normally adopted and which cannot logically be defended, is to take the movement, fighting, etc., which would normally occupy about one minute of real time, and assume that the remainder of the real time was spent in a state of frozen animation. It is totally illogical, but it works, and no one has yet found a better solution.

A further general question to be considered in

actually setting out the ships on the table is the form the playing surface will take; is there to be any kind of grid to regulate the position and movement of the ships?

In real life the movement of the ships was governed strictly by the physical laws of nature, by their design, and by the muscle power and training of their rowers. The same physical limits do not, however, apply on the wargames table, where the giant hand of the player may transport ships where he wishes. Human nature being what it is, there is a strong tendency to stretch the capabilities of ships to limits beyond their real-life potentialities, to slip them sideways in defiance of nature, to make impossibly tight turns and so forth. Even accidentally touching a ship can materially alter its position and so the course of the game.

On a plain table, realistic movement can be stimulated by accurate measurement, by the use of templates and protractors to calculate turning circles, and so forth, but while such rules satisfy the criterion of realism, they are cumbrous and time-consuming in operation, so that the time limit for the game is impossibly prolonged.

The advantage of having some form of grid is that all movement and positioning can be carried out in relation to the grid. It can be immediately seen in which direction a ship is heading, and its movement can also be defined strictly in relation to the number of grid spaces it can traverse in the period.

There are two forms of grid which can be used, one based on the square, the other on the hexagon. The square grid is easy to lay out, and has the advantage of simplicity of notation, if you want to number the squares. The difficulty with the square is that movement from square to square is distorted. If you move directly forward you move a considerably less distance than if you move diagonally.

The hexagon is less easy to mark out (although there are short cuts) but has the advantage that movement from one hexagon to another is always the same distance, so that there is never any dispute over variability of move distances.

When we are attempting the simulation of a battle such as Salamis where a large number of vessels were involved, the advantages of a grid system are manifold. It gives a quick and accurate method of moving large numbers of vessels, and ensures that the position and heading of each vessel is accurately defined. Furthermore, it forces consideration to be given to the number of ships in a given area, as a limit to the number which can occupy a certain number of grids can be laid down. This is of particular importance when we are dealing with Salamis, as the Greek tactics were dependent upon denying the Persians sufficient space for their preferred tactics, and indeed ensuring that they would have so little space that they would be in collision with themselves.

We are therefore able to summarise the means we shall use to simulate Salamis on the wargames table. It has been determined that the wargames table will not attempt to show the whole strategic area, but will only show the area of the battle, with any preliminary strategic moves being calculated beforehand on the map.

The area of play will be marked with a hexagon grid, for ease and convenience of movement.

As large a number of ships as possible will be represented, although reconstructing Salamis on a one model equals one ship basis will not be possible. (It may be noted that with most ancient naval battles this is feasible, but Salamis was an exceptionally large engagement.)

Finally, where combat is to be determined, the unit will be the ship, and there will be no attempt to calculate casualties on an individual crew basis. Thus the result of boarding will be that one ship takes another, not that so many marines are killed on one side or on another.

Let us, therefore, proceed to consider the various rules which are available, and which will apply to the reconstruction of Salamis.

12
Available Rules
and Suggested
Modifications

◆◆◆◆◆◆◆◆

There are at present three sets of published wargames rules for ancient naval warfare, which are, in order of publication:

1. Rules by Tony Bath. Tony Bath is one of the founders of modern wargaming, and also started ancient naval wargaming. Variants of his rules may be found in D. F. Featherstone's *Naval War Games*, published by Stanley Paul in 1965, and as a supplement to the Society of Ancients' *Official Wargames Rules*, which were produced by the Society in 1968. The version given in *Naval War Games* is the more complete and should now, in any case, be easier to obtain.

2. Rules by Ed. Smith. These rules appeared at the beginning of 1971, and were the first published set to use a grid, following publication of a set of rules by the present author in *Slingshot*, the journal of the Society of Ancients in 1970, based on a hexagon grid. Ed. Smith's *Rules* go into considerable detail regarding the individual ships, and therefore are less suitable for use where it is desired to represent a large number of ships.

3. Rules by the present author. An early version was published in 1970 in *Slingshot*, but a revised and improved set has now been published by the Wargames Research Group. These rules are based upon a hexagon grid, and are designed for use with a large number of ships.

The first matter to be considered with a set of rules is the type of ships which are to be represented. All the above rules permit several differing types to be used, whereas with Salamis we need only consider one type of ship, the trireme, although we will have to allow different variants of the trireme to cater for the different types of ship used by each side.

As far as Salamis is concerned we must take into account the following types of vessel:

Phoenician triremes, with high sides, faster and handier than Greek ships because of the skill of the crews.

Free Greek triremes, with lower permanent sides than the Phoenician ships, and with inferior performance.

Greeks in Persian service, with similar vessels to the free Greeks, but faster and handier because in many cases they had better crews with more skill and experience.

Other Persian ships, such as the Egyptians, etc.

These different types of ship will call for different movement rules, different vulnerability to collision, different efficiency of marines, and different reaction to losses and the result of battle. They may also be expected to react differently to weather, because of the different design of the various ships.

Most rules allocate a points value to different ships, to permit admirals to field fleets of varying composition, but allowing equally strong fleets, so that neither side will have an advantage. This is not necessary in the case of an historical battle, where the number of ships engaged is not governed by the need to create a fair Game, but by historical prototypes.

The second matter to be settled is the question of *movement* and *position* in relation to the hexagon grid.

How shall we govern the position and movement of ships? In Ed Smith's *Rules* (which use an offset rectangle which is exactly similar in effect to a hexagon) all ships but the very smallest occupy two spaces. This has the disadvantage that ships cannot realistically pivot, which was a frequent galley manoeuvre, carried out by backing water with one bank of oars and going ahead with the other bank. The aim of this manoeuvre was to keep the ship's head towards the enemy, and it could also be used to make turns tighter.

Pivoting is only possible if the ships occupy one hexagon, and thus we must allow a ship to occupy only one hexagon at any one time. In order to permit realistic forward movement, the ship must always lie with its axis at right angles to two opposing hexagon sides.

Two basic changes of position are now possible, either by *moving* forward from one hexagon to the next, or by *pivoting* 60° either clockwise or anticlockwise.

Each vessel is allowed a *Movement Factor*, say 4, expressed as 4MF. Each individual factor may be used *either* to move forward one space, *or* to pivot 60°.

It is proposed to allow the following Movement Factors to each ship:

Ships with skilled crews   5 MF
All other vessels   4 MF

In addition to forward movement, ships must be allowed to back water. Any ship can thus move up to two spaces backwards in a straight line in a period. This is instead of its normal move.

The question of *Crew fatigue* must also be taken into account, as at Salamis the Greeks were fresh, but the

Persians had been under oars all night. A ship with a tired crew has its MF reduced by 1 after the following number of MFs under oar alone:

Normal ships   32 MF
Ships with skilled crews   40 MF

As far as the Salamis reconstruction is concerned, we may take it that the Persian ships had already used up these MFs, and that all the crews were tired.

Finally on the subject of movement, it must be considered whether a ship has unlimited choice of movement options. Can a ship move forward at full speed in one period, and in the next move at full speed backwards, for instance? If movement was continuous in real as well as wargame time, this would obviously be impossible. However, since (as usual) the movement which a ship can carry out would occupy only a very small percentage of the 'real life time' represented by the wargame period, it is not considered necessary to have special rules to cover this eventuality. If they are included, then there must be, in any case, a detailed system of recording every move of every ship, and this will prove difficult with the large number of ships on the table.

All these rules relate to movement under oars only. Because of the nature of the battle of Salamis, there is no need to create special rules to cover movement under sail.

The only exception is in regard to movement under the secondary emergency sail, which was apparently used by the Corinthian division at the start of the battle. A ship may only use this sail when sailing with the wind behind the beam, and will enjoy normal move factors, although it can only go forwards, not astern, and obviously cannot stand still. It takes 1 Move Factor to raise or lower this sail.

The actual direction of the wind remains to be settled. The direction of the wind can be inferred for

Salamis – initially south, then backing round to west. While sufficient to set up a swell and permit navigation under sail, it was not sufficient to discommode the ships otherwise. The wind for wargames purposes will always blow at right angles to two hexagon sides, and as far as Salamis is concerned will be southerly for the first six periods, and will then back round to the west, one hexagon, i.e. 60°.

The only other rule necessary is one to cover the swell from the south, which is said to have particularly affected the Phoenician ships. The rule suggested to cover this is that any ship stationary with its stern to the southerly swell (first six periods of the game) must throw one die per period, with the following results:

4–6 no result
3   involuntary swing 60° port.
2   ”   ”   ”   starboard.
1   involuntary drift one space forward.

The next points to consider, following naturally on from the last rule, are the questions of ramming and of collisions.

The basic premise of the ramming rules is that any collision is likely to cause damage of some kind to either or both vessels. When relatively thin-skinned ships, such as the trireme, were rammed with the specially designed bronze ram fitted to their enemies, the problem was not making a hole, it was ensuring that the ram was accomplished with sufficient skill, so as to minimise the time the ramming ship was stationary and vulnerable. As the construction of ships tended to vary, each ship is given a *Ram Factor*, which expresses its vulnerability to ramming.

The proposed ram factors are:

Phoenician triremes   RF 1
Other triremes   RF 2

The point of giving the Phoenicians a lower RF is because their ships were probably more lightly constructed to give additional speed.

With the hexagon grid, a ship may be rammed in one of six positions, bow, port and starboard bow quarters, port and starboard stern quarters, and stern. A ram in any one of the beam positions is likely to prove fatal to the rammed ship, a ram bow to bow is likely to have no effect, a ram on the stern is likely to cripple the opponent, by destroying his steering gear.

Let us therefore set down the rules which will govern ramming in each of these positions:

Ramming bow–bow: a ship with a lower RF is crippled. If the ships ramming have equal RFs, then the ships both throw one die, and any ship throwing 1–3 is crippled.

Ramming on the bow quarter, or *on the stern quarter*: results in the rammed ship being sunk. However, provided that the ship being rammed is not crippled, and has at least as many MF as the ramming ship, it may pivot so as to take the ram on the bow (in the case of a bow quarter ram) or stern (in the case of a stern quarter ram).

A ram on the stern: means that the ship rammed is crippled.

Any accidental collision, with neither ship striking with its ram, results in both ships being crippled. This is the result when, for example, two ships drift into each other.

A collision terminates the movement of the ships involved for that period.

Only a ship ramming with the ram can break off from a ram, and must back water to do so, before pivoting and moving off. One die must be thrown, and must show 3–6 (2–6 in the case of skilled ships) for the ship to escape from the ram.

We must now turn to consideration of crippled and sunk ships.

A ship which is sunk will not in fact disappear below the waves, but will remain floating waterlogged.

A crippled ship, immediately it is hit, is made immobile, and to represent the confusion on board, its Boarding Factor (i.e. the power of its marines) will be reduced by half. At the beginning of each period one die is thrown by the ship, with the following effect:

5–6 ship recovers fully and may move unimpaired.
3–4 ship remains immobilised but regains original BF.
2 ship remains immobilised.
1 ship sinks.

All crippled and sunk ships will drift one space directly downwind each period.

Boarding is next to be considered. It has already been decided that there will be no special attempt to represent the various types of marines other than by a factor, which we may call the Boarding Factor, which will vary from ship to ship. The special types of marine which we have to consider are as follows:

1. Greek hoplites supported by other troops, as on the free Greek ships.

2. Greek hoplites and Persian bow and spear men, as in many of the Persian vessels.

3. Egyptian marines and Persian bow and spear men, as in the Egyptian fleet.

4. Other types of troops and Persian bow and spear men, as in the rest of the Persian contingents.

The Boarding Factor (BF) which is allocated to each of these types is as follows:

Greek Hoplites	4
Greek Hoplites/Persian troops	3
Egyptian marines/Persian troops	3
Other troops/Persian troops	2

Any ship which is in contact with another may board. Both ships then throw one die and add it to the appropriate BF. If the result is two higher than the opponent's score, the opponent is taken. If not, there is no result.

It may arise that one side has more than one ship in contact with the enemy. In this case all the BFs are added together, and one die is thrown for all the ships on the one side involved; the result obtained is binding upon all the ships involved in the mêlée in question.

A ship wishing to break off from a mêlée can do so if its bows are in contact with the enemy, or if it has just had a higher boarding score (die plus BF).

A ship which has been captured may be moved by its captors at a speed of 2 MF per period.

A prize may be taken by any vessel which moves

Fig. 23. Wargame rules in practice. Here is a very simple illustration to clarify the basic operation of the rules:

1. Movement
Ships A and B are Egyptian triremes with RF of 2; ships C and D are Phoenician with RF of 1. Ships W, X, Y and Z are Greeks with RF of 2. All ships have MF of 4, except C and D whose MF is 5.

Ships A, B, W and X each move forward 2 spaces using 2 MF, and then each uses a third MF to ram the opponent ahead in the bows. Ship D backs water 1 space, using its move to do so. Ship C moves forward 2 spaces. Ship Y also moves forward 2 spaces and ship Z moves forward 2 spaces and pivots 60°, menacing a ram on C's bow quarter (Z has used 3 MF). Ship C chooses to pivot to meet Z and does so. Ship Z then rams C in bows, and ship Y rams C in bow quarter.

2. Results of ramming
Ships A, B, W and X each throw 1 die, getting respectively 2, 6, 4 and 3. Ships A and X are therefore crippled. Ship C had a lower RF than ship Z and is thus automatically crippled, while ship Z is automatically unharmed. In addition, ship C is, of course, sunk by ship Y's ram in the bow quarter.

3. Boarding
Ships A and W, and B and X board each other; dice are thrown:

Ship	A versus	W	B versus	X
BF	1 (cripple)	4	3	2 (crippled)
die	4	6	3	3
total	5	10	6	5
result	W takes A		No result	

4. Reaction
Ships A, B, C and D now constitute a minus squadron, and must throw 1 die for reaction. The die is 4, plus 2 for 2 plus ships, minus 2 for 2 minus ships in own squadron, minus 1 for enemy plus squadron. The final result is thus 3, and the Persian squadron must retire out of reach of the enemy.

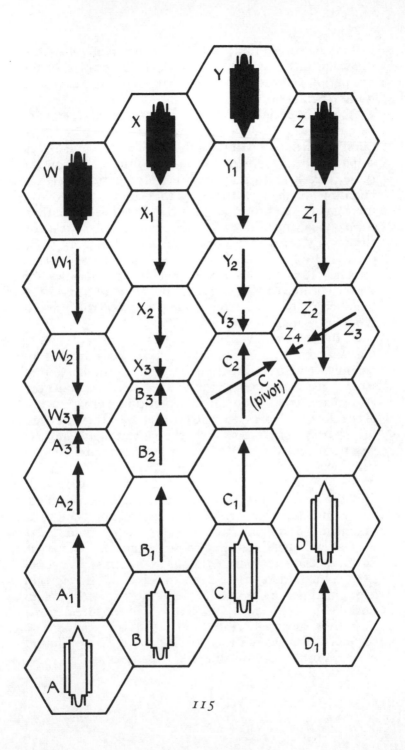

within one space of it, provided that no enemy is within the same distance. Both vessels remain stationary for one period and the recovered prize then fights as before for its original side.

Only two special factors applying to Salamis remain to be considered, in regard to boarding. The first is the question of the *apobathra* with which all the free Greek ships may be presumed to have been fitted. To allow for these, Greek ships may be given one extra BF when boarding an enemy with whom they are in contact with their bows. The other factor is the question of archery. As has been mentioned in the chapter on tactics, the ships were not well designed for massed archery to be used, and all ships had screens to protect crews from missiles. It is thus assumed that no special rules for archery need to be allowed, and the effect of it has been included in the Boarding Factors allowed to different types of troops.

At the tactical level, the only remaining question is that of command organisation. For the purposes of Salamis, it will be sufficient to organise the fleets into fairly large components, for the Persians based on the Phoenician and Ionian contingents, plus perhaps a few of the fleet of Cyprus, for the Greeks the Athenian fleet, the Spartans and their allies, the Corinthians, and the Aeginetan squadron. Of these various units, the Persian ships will all be skilled in the Ionian and Phoenician fleets, but all the crews will be tired. Of the Greek fleet, only the Aeginetan squadron can be considered skilled.

A commander for each of these separate units must be designated, and in addition a fleet flagship would under normal circumstances have to be designated. However, in the special situation prevailing at Salamis, no overall fleet commanders have been specified. The Persian supreme commander was Xerxes, who was sitting on an unsinkable rock viewing the battle, and the Greek command was effectively vested in the unit commanders, so the loss of Eurybiadas was not likely to have a profound effect on other than his immediate command.

Each of the commanders of the various fleets is assumed to have a specially skilled crew, and so adds one to all factors at all times.

The main purpose of specifying the squadron organisation is to provide a basis for determining *morale*, and the effect of the casualties which are bound to be suffered in the course of the battle. For the purposes of morale, each ship is counted as either plus or minus. A minus ship is a crippled ship, a captured ship, a sunk ship, a ship under sail (unless as part of a specific ruse) or a ship more than three spaces from its squadron. A plus ship is any other ship.

To determine morale, a test is taken. This test must be taken on the following occasions:

1. On any occasion when the squadron in question comes within five spaces of an enemy, the whole squadron having previously been more than five spaces away from any enemy.

2. When the squadron has less plus than minus ships, and at each subsequent loss.

3. When the squadron leader becomes minus.

4. When an adjacent squadron becomes minus.

The method of taking the test is as follows. Two dice are thrown (one die by squadrons with a majority of minus ships), and the following additions and deductions are made:

Add one for: each plus ship in squadron, each friendly plus squadron, each enemy minus squadron.

Subtract one for: each minus ship in squadron, each friendly minus squadron, each enemy plus squadron.

If the resulting dice score is over six, the squadron in question is unaffected. If the result is less than six, the squadron must retire at least five spaces from the nearest enemy ship and not approach closer until a reaction in excess of six has been obtained in the test, which may be taken voluntarily at the start of any period. If the result of the test is 0 or less, the squadron must hoist sail (if possible) and in any case retreat off the table to its own base. Ships menaced with boarding or ramming by an enemy, and who cannot escape, will immediately surrender.

This concludes the various tactical rules which will be necessary to fight the battle of Salamis on the tactical level. It remains for the strategic rules to be considered. These will be used to carry out any night moves necessary and to work out the general movements of ships prior to the battle.

The strategic rules need not be very elaborate. All that is needed is for a simple rule to be laid down for movement of ships as any fighting will be transferred to a wargames table. We may assume that any fleet cruising will have moved at about three knots, and at least once in a 24 hour period will have needed to come to shore to replenish water and, more particularly, to rest the rowers.

In this particular case the strategic moves were calculated on an Admiralty chart (No. 1657 'Saronikos Kolpos') with a scale of 1 : 100,000. Small plastic blocks were used to represent the ships, 20 × 5 × 5 mm representing 100 ships, and smaller blocks pro rata. This is exactly correct for 100 ships in three ranks with 60 yds. intervals, giving a frontage of 2,000 yds.

On this basis, a unit was permitted to move at a rate of 60 mm per hour on the chart (the time being split into one hour periods) and an additional hour was required for any special movements, such as attempting to pass a strait requiring a major formation change, manning ship and putting to sea, or landing and beaching.

The main danger to be guarded against in this type of strategic wargame would be weather, but in fact the conditions were good at the time of Salamis, so this can be ignored. If an attempt had been made to fight Artemisium on the same method, then it would have been necessary to frame rules for weather.

13
Setting up
Salamis
as a Wargame

◇◆◇◆◇◆◇◆◇

We must now consider the practical problems involved in setting up Salamis as a wargame. The basic requirements which must be provided are a table, with a playing surface marked in hexagon grids, suitable terrain to indicate the distinctive land areas of the Salamis area, and sufficient ships. Also required will be dice, and paper and pencil for recording the few essential facts necessary.

The first essential is the table, and in this particular case, it was decided to make a permanent playing surface, so an ordinary table could not be directly used. The decision was made to reproduce Salamis with ships on a 1–for–12 basis, with one representing 12 in the original battle. This meant, first, that the playing area could be fairly small, and second, that a number of variant games could be played in a fairly short time, so as to try out all the various permutations and combinations.

The basis of the field of play was accordingly taken as a piece of ordinary hardboard, 42 × 33 in., and the size of hexagon selected was 1.2 in. diameter, measured from opposing apexes.

It was calculated that this size of hexagon, containing one ship model supposed to represent 12 ships three deep and four abreast, would represent to scale an area about 250 yds. in diameter.

To facilitate preparation of the hexagon gridded board, an area of hexagons of the appropriate size was drawn out on graph paper. Hexagons may be readily drawn on any squared paper, bearing in mind that the relationship of the diameter between apexes, the diameter between parallel sides, and the length of any side have the approximate relationship of length 12:10:6, or whatever variant gives a convenient method of measurement with the paper selected.

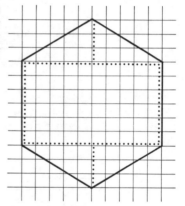

Fig. 24. Drawing a hexagon on squared paper. A rectangle 6 squares × 10 squares is extended 3 squares up and down from the centre of the long sides.

To draw the hexagons, assuming a side of six squares, first mark a series of parallel lines, six squares long, ten squares apart. Then mark the points on the graph paper midway between the parallel sides and three squares above or below them respectively. Finally join up these points to the ends of the lines originally drawn, and you have one row of hexagons of the desired size. Repeat this as desired to give the area of hexagons needed.

In the present case, a photocopier was used to make a series of sheets all from the original master hexagon grid, and these sheets were glued to the hardboard, giving the appropriate area of gridded sea.

The next question was the matter of terrain. Most wargamers, whether on land or sea, find it more convenient to use portable terrain, which may be moved as required for a particular battle, and which does not limit the players to any particular set layout. One of the most effective methods of creating terrain now is to use the tiles and blocks of expanded polystyrene which are widely available from decorators shops. These may be easily cut to any desired shape, and, painted with an acrylic paint, make the most realistic terrain.

However, for Salamis it was decided that provided that the line of the coast was clearly marked, a properly contoured terrain could be dispensed with, and in fact the terrain was simply marked on the board accurately, and was then painted in with acrylic paint. The final result was an accurate representation of the Salamis strait in two dimensions only, but it was entirely satisfactory for the purposes of the reconstruction.

This was for the tactical part of the game; for the strategic part, as stated earlier, the sole requirement was the standard Admiralty chart.

The next problem to be overcome was the question of ships, and here the ancient naval wargamer runs into a problem, because there are not currently on sale model ships which can be used for ancient naval wargaming without modification. The ships which are required for Salamis should not have masts and sails, but should have oars extended, and at present there are not the commercial figures available to conform to this requirement. The ship models which have been produced either have masts and sails but no oars, or have neither masts nor oars, and are simply bare hulls.

There are two choices therefore, for the wargamer. Either he converts commercial models, or he makes his own. To refight Salamis ships of both types were employed.

The conversion of commercial models first, then. To start, remove the mast and sail, if integrally cast with the hull, and file the deck flush. If at any stage it is desired to show the model with a mast and sail, it is better to drill a hole through the hull into which a pin or wire mast of your own construction can be inserted. Not only is this removable at will, but is very much stronger than the cast soft metal of the commercial ship.

The basic hull is now ready for the oars. Most models do not show the outrigger in sufficient detail; as may be seen from the three view drawings earlier in this book; this was in fact a prominent feature. However, should you wish to show it, a balsa strip of suitable length and width fixed to the hull sides and made flush with the deck is quite suitable.

The next stage is the provision of oars. This involves not only the oars themselves, but also a base on which they may rest, which is on the level of the ship's waterline, and is in fact painted to represent the sea. If the oars are simply left unsupported, they will be too fragile to withstand the handling which will be necessary when they are used for wargame purposes.

Of course it is not necessary to make any attempt to model the individual oars; in the case of a trireme at 1:1200 scale, this would involve 150 minute oars somewhat over one tenth of an inch long, which the most dedicated modeller might find a task beyond his powers. A general fault of commercial models, where they attempt to show any kind of rows of oars, is to make the oars far too big, and too few for the scale.

All that is needed is a block or card to represent the mass of oars. Cut to the shape of the oarbank, it may conveniently be fixed to the ship's side at the point where the uppermost oars would emerge, and be fixed again to the base which has been added to the model, representing the level of the water. Card, thin balsa or plastic card may all be used for this operation, but plastic card has the best combination of thinness and strength.

Somewhat similar in style is the method of building ship models from scratch. The method recommended is very simple, and a large number of ships which are quite satisfactory from the wargames point of view can

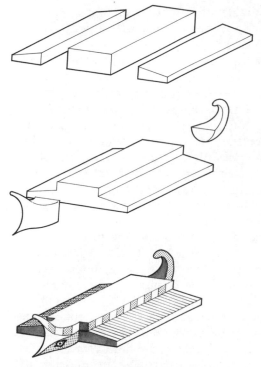

Fig. 25. *A simple scratch-built trireme.*
Top: *Centre section and oarbanks of balsa strip.*
Middle: *Carved bow and stern sections.*
Bottom: *Paint finished model.*

be built within a very short length of time.

The essential is a series of strips of balsa of varying dimensions, corresponding respectively to the hull and outrigger centre section, the bow and stern sections, and the oar banks. For the first two you will require a rectangular section of wood, while for the oar bank the strip sold for aeromodellers as 'trailing edge' (which has a wedge shaped section), is best.

The method of construction is based upon cutting to scale a series of lengths of the hull and outrigger centre section. To these on either side are cemented the oarbanks, which are slightly less in length than the hull centre section. Finally the bow and stern sections, which have to be separately shaped, are added, and the model is complete except for painting.

On the question of painting of the ships, a few words are necessary. Either oil-based paints or the acrylic water-based paints may be employed, but only practice will show which colour schemes look most effective.

Triremes were, like most ancient shipping, colourful and decorative craft, but on the small scale model available, it is not possible to show in great detail the necessary degree of decoration, which must therefore be suggested. In any case the wargamer tends to view his models from above, whereas they were in real life usually seen from water level.

In general, it is best first to paint the model all over black. The deck area is then painted ochre, and the oarbanks and the sea an appropriate sea colour, such as blue green. This is the basic colour scheme, which will serve for all the ships.

Using either pen or brush, the rowing benches and central gangway may be marked on the deck area, and the oars added to the oarbank by the same method. This gives the most effective looking oars; the author originally used black oarbanks, with the oars picked out in yellow or white paint, but the black oars on natural sea, which is a style of painting used by Phil Barker, is, in general, superior.

At the sea level, the movement of the oars in the water may be suggested by painting foam round the blades, and foam round the bows of the model also looks effective.

The main points by which a ship may be distinguished from its fellows are now to be included, and it is suggested that the area of the railing from bow to stern should be painted one base colour, which is carried round up the curved stern. Stripes, spots, or a chequered effect can be added to this in different colours, and it will be found that colour coding systems for the different squadrons of a model fleet can be readily devised. In addition to this, an identification number on the deck of each ship is a material help, in the course of a battle, to distinguish the ships one from another. Such numbers, self adhesive, can be bought from stationers or from photographic suppliers, and if bought in this form can be readily removed as desired.

At any rate, the wargamer has now aquired his rival fleets.

To complete the requirements he needs only dice and some means of keeping suitable records of the battle. The dice are simple to obtain and will be in the possession of any wargamer; the rules proposed do not require the use of the average 2 3 3 4 4 5 dice which are often called for in sets of rules.

The requirements of the record system can be solved without difficulty by the use of one sheet for each fleet. This should show the various ships in the fleet, with appropriate columns to give their current status, the number of periods under oar (to indicate whether they are yet hampered by tired crew) etc. A specimen of such a sheet, for the Salamis wargame, is shown, giving details of the Greek fleet, in a period just before the battle began.

The various columns are as shown in the Ship Record Sheet reproduced on page 126.

Ship number and reference: this is purely for identification purposes, so that the ships may be clearly identified on the table. In this case no names have been given to the ships, only an indication of nationality.

Ship type: all the Greek ships are, naturally, Greek triremes; since the composition of the Persian fleet varied and some of the Persian ships were lighter than others, this column was of more value for that fleet. The different types in the Persian fleet also had different BFs.

Crew: this is purely to indicate the standard of crew training, which governed the MFs which the ships had. The Aeginetans are a crack unit with skilled crews, and so obtain higher MFs under the rules.

Sails and sail status: these columns are to indicate if

Ship Record Sheet

Ship Number and Reference	Ship Type	Crew	Sails	Sail Status	MF's Used Under Oar	Current Status
1 Athens Flag	Greek Trireme	Trained	Not Aboard		16	OK
2 Athens	"	"	"		15	OK
3 "	"	"	"		15	OK
4 "	"	"	"		16	OK
5 "	"	"	"		17	OK
6 "	"	"	"		17	OK
7 "	"	"	"		16	OK
8 "	"	"	"		15	OK
9 "	"	"	"		15	OK
10 "	"	"	"		15	OK
11 "	"	"	"		16	OK
12 "	"	"	"		16	OK
13 Aegina Flag	"	Skilled	"		16	OK
14 Aegina	"	"	"		16	OK
15 Aegina	"	"	"		16	OK
16 Sparta Flag	"	Trained	"		15	OK
17 Corinth Flag	"	"	Aboard	Hoisted	6	OK
18 Corinth	"	"	"	"	6	OK
19 Corinth	"	"	"	"	6	OK
20 Argolid	"	"	Not Aboard		15	OK
21 Euboea	"	"	"		15	OK
22 Colonists of Corinth	"	"	"		16	OK
23 Sicyon	"	"	"		16	OK
24 Megara	"	"	"		16	OK
25 Megara	"	"	"		16	OK
26 Aegean	"	"	"		16	OK

the sails are on board and if so whether they are hoisted or not.

MFs used under oars: this will give an indication of the stage at which the crew become tired. Most of the ships still have half the full value MFs left, with the exception of the Corinthians, who are under sail and so have not used their oarsmen to any extent.

Current status: this is largely blank at present because the battle has yet to begin in earnest; it is primarily intended to record such matters as whether the ship is crippled or sunk, and how far it has recovered from its crippling.

It is convenient if the Record Sheet can be covered by plastic sheet, so that a chinagraph pencil can be used to make the entries; this means that the Record Sheet can be used as often as required.

14
Description
of the Wargame
◇◆◇◆◇◆◇◆◇◆◇

The terrain and the method of setting up the rival fleets have been described, and we may now proceed to the description of the wargame itself. As the battle is being reproduced on a basis of one ship model equals twelve ships in the original battle, the numbers of the opposing fleets were as follows:

	Original numbers	models
Greek fleet:		
Athenian squadron	160	13
Aeginetan squadron	30	3
Corinthian squadron	40	3
Spartans and other Greeks	80	7
	310	26
Persian fleet:		
Fleet of Phoenicia	150	12
Fleet of Ionia	150	12
Rump of Fleet of Cyprus	50	4
	350	28

It will be noted that the Egyptian squadron has not

been represented, although it was represented in the strategic game beforehand.

The original strategic moves were first played out, and the following position emerged. The Persian picket line opposite the eastern straits which consisted of the Phoenician and Ionian fleets, plus the balance of the fleet of Cyprus, was in position within three hours, but it took over six to get a fleet from the Phaleron area round to cover the western straits. The effect of this was that a fleet once sent to the western strait could not effectively intervene in the main battle. Furthermore, it would take almost a similar period for such a fleet to circumnavigate the island round the north and appear in the Greek rear in the western straits.

More important, it was clear that provided the Persians started to make their move, and obtained an hour or two of start, as they would with a secret move, they could in fact block both the western and eastern exits before the Greeks could get ships out and past them. It might have been possible for a few isolated stragglers to have got past, but not the main body of the fleet. The Persian move, as a blocking operation, would therefore have been successful against any Greek attempted breakout, provided that the Persians had the element of surprise.

The behaviour of the Corinthian squadron was also illuminated, as it was found that it would take nearly half the day to get as far as the western straits. Thus if the Egyptians did try to enter the western straits, the Corinthians might not be expected to intercept before the enemy entered the bay of Eleusis. However, if the Corinthian squadron were more skilled than the Egyptians (which is certainly possible) they might hope to delay them sufficiently to prevent them intervening in the main battle. In the event, the Corinthians were advised that the Persian western force had not entered the straits, apparently, and so were able to turn back.

The question of the strategic moves having thus been covered, we must turn to the deployment of the ships on the wargames board.

In fact, three separate alternatives were tried out as wargames: first of all with both fleets in their dawn positions, which developed into a wargame just north of Psyttaleia, as described in the chapter on the battle; second, a wargame with the Persians nearly on the Greek beaches, which is the favourite modern interpretation, and third (just to see what would happen), an attempted Greek breakout against the Persian cordon disposed south of Psyttaleia.

First then, what of the battle north of Psyttaleia. The Persians were disposed in their cordon five or six hexagons below the island, with the 12 ships of the Persian flotilla forming the left wing, and the 16 ships of the Ionian and Cypriot fleets forming the right. The ships used for the Persian fleet were mainly Minifigs biremes, which were somewhat larger than the Decalset ships which represented the Greek fleet. One or two scratch built balsa wood ships were also used, however, to form the Persian fleet.

The Greek fleet was disposed on its beaches, with the three ships of the Aeginetan squadron in Ambelaki Bay, the main fleet on the central beaches, and the Corinthians on the northernmost beach.

The initial moves were then made, each side moving alternately, with the Greeks moving first; combat was adjudicated after both sides had moved.

Because of the time/ground scale, it was found almost at once that the initial deployments were taking far longer than in the actual battle. In fact the actual battle did not commence until period eight, which is well into the afternoon under the normal method of calculation of time. First to reach their battle positions were the Aeginetans, partly because, as skilled crews, they had an extra MF each period, partly because they had the least distance to go from their base.

The main feature of the deployment was the time taken for the Persian fleet to deploy through the gaps either side of Psyttaleia. The leading ships were able to reach the northern line of the isle by the end of the third period, but then had to halt in order to enable the ships following them to catch up. This was particularly marked with the Phoenician fleet west of the island, where most of the ships had a change of direction to contend with. The Ionian fleet had a rather easier task in the eastern gap, but a similar delay was needed to permit their stragglers to catch up.

Surprisingly, the Greek deployment took an almost equal period, but both sides had themselves into a reasonable position by the eighth period; the Persian columns were closed up, but not fully deployed, while the Greeks were in line facing south.

The general engagement then ensued, with the Greek ships advancing to attack both the Phoenician and the Ionian fleets. In the first ramming moves (which could not be avoided by the Persian fleet) the leading Phoenician triremes, which had a RF of one as opposed to the two of the other ships present were all crippled. However the dice went against the Greeks in the subsequent boarding actions, because only one of the Phoenician ships was taken by boarding. The Phoenician ships had a BF of two as opposed to the Greek four, and this was reduced to one because they were crippled, but even this differential was insufficient to permit the Greeks to take as many as they might have done.

The Ionian front was much wider, as they had had a wider gap to come through, and had had more time to deploy. Since their RFs were the same as those of the Greeks facing them, there was no automatic crippling on contact bow to bow, which was determined by throw of dice. Again the dice gave an unrepresentative result, as only one ship on either side was crippled, instead of the 50 per cent which should be the average, under the rules adopted. Since the BFs of the two opposing units were four to three, there was less statistical likelihood of ships being taken automatically by boarding, and in fact only two of the Ionian ships were so taken.

So far, therefore, the Persian fleet had held its position, although far weaker than the Greeks under the circumstances. In the next period, however, they began to run into difficulties. Part of the problem was the special rule whereby stationary ships were likely to be shifted by the southerly wind and swell; three of the Ionian ships were crippled by their own side in this way, and one of the Phoenicians'. Also affecting the Phoenicians was the fact that they were fighting on two sides, and one of their ships was sunk by the Aeginetans. Finally the dice favoured the Greeks in the boarding actions against the Ionians.

The result was that both the Phoenician and Ionian fleets had a majority of minus ships after this round of fighting and were compelled to throw a reaction. In both cases the result was not sufficient to permit them to do more than retreat five paces from the nearest enemy.

This meant that the leading ships, which were mostly crippled and unable to escape, surrendered, while the ships behind turned and attempted to make their way out back past the island of Psyttaleia.

The Greek pursuit was seriously hampered by the prizes and cripples, which not only formed a solid wall in front of them, but were also drifting slowly north-wards, or would have been if the Greek line had not been in the way! On the Ionian front, where the ships were not so congested, some of the Greek ships succeeded in getting through to pursue, but the survivors of the Cypriot and Phoenician fleets made an unhampered getaway.

The final result of the battle was as follows:

Persian fleet	Ships	Actual equivalent	lost	Actual equivalent
Phoenicians	12	150	7	84
Ionians	12	150	10	120
Cypriots	4	50	1	12
	28	350	18	216
Greek fleet	26	310	3	36

These figures are very close to the reported losses for

each side in the original battle, and the Persian fleet was unable to do much at all, because of the inferiority of its position. In fact this particular simulation was a massacre rather than a reasonable game.

The second simulation which was played out, placed the Persian fleet well up on the Greek beaches. In fact the original deployments were not adhered to, because it would have meant that the Greeks were inactive on their own beaches for most of the day while the Persians crept nearer and nearer! Rather, the ships were laid out with the opposing fleets in a position immediately before action commenced.

This simulation was even more of a massacre than the previous alternative tried, because the Persians were being effectively attacked from more than one side, and it was relatively easy for two Greek ships to attack one Persian, one feinting to ram bow to bow, or actually doing so and risking the cripple, and the other then ramming and sinking by hitting the bow quarter. The Persian losses in this option were disastrous, because the Aeginetan squadron was attacking the tail of their line. Here it swiftly had success, and the upshot was that the crippled and sunken ships which resulted drifted northwards, so that within a period or two the line of retreat of the entire Persian fleet was entirely blocked by a line of cripples and waterlogged hulks. Again Greek losses were few, while the Persians were entirely eliminated.

The third simulation was more of an exercise to test the rules than as a practical strategic alternative, or an attempt to show what might have happened, or what really did happen, unbeknown to the ancient and modern historians. This was a breakout by the Greek fleet through the Persian cordon.

The assumption behind this alternative was that the Greeks were in fact in disarray, and were planning to break out; it also presupposed that this attempt was made immediately after dawn, and that the Greek fleet had moved as far as Psyttaleia during the hours of darkness.

The initial starting positions were accordingly as follows. The Persian fleet was as for the start of the first game, with a long cordon about six hexagons south of Psyttaleia. The Phoenician fleet had its left flank resting on the island of Salamis, while the Ionian right wing was on Munychia, and this left a gap in the centre of the cordon, about three hexagons wide.

The Greek fleet was deployed with the Athenians on the left wing, facing south in the eastern exit from the straits, while the rest of the Greek fleet was in the exit to the west of Psyttaleia. The Corinthian squadron was leading, followed by Sparta and her allies, and the Aeginetan squadron was in line astern covering the right flank of the Greek array.

The Athenians formed line abreast and attacked the Ionians, both fleets being evenly matched, and met head on in a great boarding battle. In fact the dice more than made up for their earlier capriciousness, with all the ships on both sides except two being crippled! This meant that both sides were in an overall minus situation, and both had to throw reactions, which meant each retiring more than five spaces from the nearest enemy. In effect, therefore, the Greeks on either side had fought themselves to a standstill, and the Athenians had to retire within the straits, their breakout attempt having failed.

The course of events was more complicated on the other flank. While the Ionians and Athenians were engaged with each other, the Cypriots on the left flank of the Ionians had veered to the left to close the gap which the Spartans were attempting to break through. These ships met the Corinthians head on while the main fleet of the Phoenicians came in on the flank. The Aeginetans in the meantime attempted to break away round the extreme left flank of the Phoenicians, and four of the Phoenician ships were detached to deal with them, which they did with some success, trapping two out of the three ships against the coast of Salamis. Thus only one escaped. In the meantime one of the Corinthian vessels in the centre succeeded in getting past the Cypriots, but the rest were held, and with open water and numerical superiority the Persian left wing was able to take or sink all the ships in this part of the battle.

The final conclusion of this action was therefore:

	Total ships	Original equivalent	Losses	Original equivalent
Phoenicians	12	150	2	24
Cypriots	4	50	—	—
Ionians	12	150	11	132
Persian Total	28	350	13	156
Athenians	13	150	11	132
Others	13	160	11	132
Greek Total	26	310	22	264

Most of the Ionian and Athenian losses represent crippled ships, which would under normal circumstances have been quickly repaired, but the losses to the rest of the Greeks represent total losses.

The result of this simulation was that the Greeks were heavily defeated, with half the fleet lost, and the damaged remainder being confined once more in the Salamis strait. The difference now was that the Persians could, with the numerical superiority they now enjoyed, enter the straits and destroy the Athenians at their anchorage, if they did not choose to fight, or alternatively split their fleet, so that a good proportion of it could mask the Athenians, while the remainder supported the Persian army on its attack on the Isthmus of Corinth.

15
How Realistic
a Simulation?

◇◆◇◆◇◆◇◆◇

At first sight, the wargame which has just been described offers a very realistic simulation of the battle of Salamis; the Greeks have won, and the respective casualties correspond closely with the recorded figures. However, it may just be that the result has been realistic because there were various irregularities in the game rules which have favoured now one side, now the other, and have merely cancelled one another out. There is also the possibility that the rules have given the same result as the battle because they have been so based on the original that no other result is possible.

It was to check against the latter possibility that the effect of the Greeks trying to break out, and having to fight the Persians in open water, was played out. The effect of this was so convincing a Persian victory that the general realism of the rules may be accepted.

We must still, however, examine the course of the battle as reconstructed on the wargames table, to see if any inconsistencies or improbabilities may be found.

The first is evident: in the original battle the action

began soon after dawn, whereas in our simulation it was not till midday that the battle properly began. The result of the time scale adopted is bound to give a similar effect in any battle, unless the fleets are drawn up in their pre-battle positions, because the fastest ships can only pass through five spaces in any one period, which is equivalent to about 1200 yds. in an hour, or a speed of slightly over ½ knot. This is only about a tenth of the speed a good trireme should have been able to maintain for an hour.

While it would certainly be possible to speed up the game to adhere to a more realistic timetable, by allowing much longer opening moves, until within sight or a certain distance from an enemy vessel, the difficulty likely to be created by making the opening moves longer is to create unreality in the deployment. The main danger is that one side or the other will be allowed to occupy a position which they would not otherwise have reached if there had been strict accountability of time.

On the whole it is better to adhere to the original moves, and perhaps allow a shortening of the timescale per period in the opening moves. If the opening movement periods were stated to take only ten minutes instead of one hour, the speed of the models would approximate more realistically to the historical prototype, and since periods in which no fighting takes place are quick to play, the foreshortening of the timescale would still not prevent the game taking a reasonable time to play in real life.

Again on the timescale, it will be noted that while the deployment of the opposing fleets took several times as long as it should have done, the actual battle was very much shorter than the original action. The reason for this is the need for one model to represent twelve original ships. As a result, everything happens on a greatly speeded-up basis.

This is primarily because of the depth of the formation which is represented. One ship represents twelve, but twelve ships in a formation four broad and three ships deep. When therefore a Phoenician model rams a Greek model head on, and is crippled, it is as if twelve ships were crippled all at once. This may well not be unhistoric. As we may expect Phoenician vessels to have been more lightly built than Greek vessels, they will have been vulnerable to being crippled. Bow to bow ramming tended to place each vessel's stem on to the cross timbers at the front of the outrigger of the other ship, and those of the lighter ship were likely to suffer damage, weakening the outrigger and so the oarpower. If therefore the model were to represent twelve ships in single line abreast, then for the model to be crippled would simply represent a short cut to what happened in real life.

When, however, two real life formations met in the circumstances, it would not be twelve ships which were crippled, but only four, because the front ranks consisted of four ships only. The second and third ranks have not yet been engaged. Where in the wargame the Persian fleet was three or four models deep, in real life it was nine to twelve ships deep, and only ten per cent of the ships involved were in action.

The wargame therefore is unreal in that it tends to make the action too fast and creates a situation where the Greeks tend to be too effective too fast. The solution to this problem would be to wargame on a basis of one equals one, or one equals three ships in line abreast, and with most battles this would be the solution adopted. In the particular circumstances of Salamis the numbers prevented this being carried out.

Again in the real battle once the two forces had met it will have been difficult for the two sides to get at each other, once the leading lines had met and the resulting boarding actions had been fought out. Even where ships were sunk, taken or crippled, lack of room to move will have prevented their being shifted to enable the vessels behind to get on to attack new targets. This was certainly a factor properly reproduced in the rules, but it only became effective after the battle was won, and prevented the Greeks organising an effective pursuit. This also would be solved to some extent by fighting on a larger scale, with one model representing fewer original ships.

However, it may be fairly claimed that while the rules have tended to foreshorten this part of the battle, they have not made a final result which has been unhistorical.

It may further be said in defence of the rules and the simulation which has been played that the relation of real time to wargame time is the main problem involved in any wargame situation, and no really satisfactory solution has yet been found.

Apart from problems of timescale, some limitations on freedom of action have inevitably been posed by the use of the hexagonal grid. One of the main difficulties has been that it is not possible to make fine adjustments of course, as the minimum turn which can be made is 60°. This is a positive advantage in some situations, and in the case of the Salamis wargame is not the disadvantage it might be if the models were on a 1:1 basis. It might be objected that with the method of turning adopted, for instance, too much way is lost. Again, the fact that models represent more than one ship is of importance here. The loss of way on the turn might be a relevant criticism where one model equals one ship, but where the model represents, as here, twelve, then the difficulty of keeping twelve ships in formation through turns should not be exaggerated. And even where one model does equal one ship, the loss of way on the turn is realistic, especially in the battle conditions when oars may be expected to have been used for positioning as much as the big steering oars.

A further possible source of criticism is that the hexagon grid makes for inflexibility in the number of ships per yard of front. This is to a certain extent true, in that an infinite variability of front cannot be created. But certainly the effect of trying to get too many ships into a confined space is reproduced on a large scale: the Persians had no room for any kind of manoeuvre, and the Greeks did.

While therefore there are points on which the rules

necessarily have to diverge to some extent from real life, they still give a realistic result, and we may fairly claim therefore that the simulation is a realistic one.

What further points of interest arise from the war-games fought, once we accept that the simulations are realistic? Perhaps what is most of interest is not the simulation based on what we believe to have happened, but the wargames fought on other suggested variants, such as the battle up by the Greek beaches, or the attempted Greek breakout.

The battle fought up by the Greek beaches, for instance, shows up two major objections to the theory that it was here that the battle took place in reality. The first is the great disparity in time involved between the Greek fleet reaching their positions and the Persians getting up the straits from their proposed cordon. To have reached such a position within a reasonable time after dawn, the Persians must already have been coming into the straits before dawn, and this is something we are assured did not occur.

The second objection is to the course of the battle, and may be taken in two parts. First is why the Persians should put themselves into such a disastrous position, and should, for instance, not advance on a broad front, and attack the Aeginetans. While they may have been lured on by over confidence, their advance will have tended to spread out if they were pressing forward uncontrollably, and this will have tended to spread the front, not contract it. Further, if they were uncontrollably confident, why did they not move to attack all the forces facing them?

And if they finally did get into such a poor position, the wargame showed that it was most improbable that they would have been able to withdraw any of their ships. If their flank and rear was attacked, it would soon have been blocked by the cripples and sunken ships, and it would have been physically impossible for the remainder of the fleet to have broken back and fled. Again, if the Persians had been surrounded in such a bad position, their natural reaction in a panic would not have been to try to break out by sea, but to run ashore and abandon the ships. There are plenty of examples of individual crews and fleets abandoning their ships and retiring to a friendly shore, some from earlier in the very same Salamis campaign.

The wargame simulation may therefore claim to have confirmed the implausibility of this particular reconstruction of the battle.

Equally interesting was the simulation of the action which resulted from an attempted Greek breakout. Where the Greeks met another force on relatively level terms, as was the case with the Athenian fleet encountering the Ionians, then a result similar to the third day at Artemisium was achieved; no decisive result, but a stand off. Where a superior fleet was able to encounter an inferior with room to manoeuvre, as was the case with the Phoenicians and the Spartans, then the inferior Greek fleet was wiped out.

This tends to confirm the validity of the rules, but also shows what would have happened had the Greek fleet not been in the hands of first class commanders, and had they not had the benefit of the skilful planning of Themistocles to bring about a battle on terms where the lesser fleet in all but boarding ability had everything in its favour.

16
The Salamis Campaign as a Strategic Game

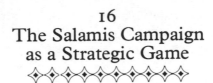

In addition to the tactical and strategic rules already considered, it is worth examining in greater detail alternative methods of reconstructing the Salamis campaign. One of the simplest and most attractive is to fight it as a board game, with the clash between rival forces being either transferred to the wargames table and fought out in full, or settled by a simple means of resolving combat without using ship or troop models. A combination of these methods is recommended to the naval wargamer who wants a realistic campaign, but does not, for example, want to be involved in land battles.

The method adopted for fighting the strategic game was a combination of the techniques used by board wargamers, together with the control methods used, for instance, by Tony Bath, doyen of Ancient wargamers, in his longstanding and well known Hyborian campaign.

Board wargames normally involve movement and definition of the position of units on a grid (nowadays usually a hexagon grid) with definite rules governing movement and terrain. In the peculiar circumstances of

Fig. 26. Sketch map of Central Greece, showing the areas of importance in the map campaign.

the Salamis campaign, these were not considered necessary. The landscape of Greece is separated as a general rule into flat plains of varying size bounded by mountains and rough terrain, and fighting is therefore likely only at certain clearly identifiable points. In the plains the Persians would be able to deploy fully, bringing their vast numerical superiority into play, and more important, allowing their cavalry to take a full part. The experience of the Plataea campaign in the year following Salamis was that Greek armies of this period had no answer to cavalry in open country. Equally, in hilly or mountainous terrain, the superior Greek hand-to-hand capabilities could be employed on a narrow front with every hope of success.

Similar considerations apply to the naval part of the campaign, since the numerous islands and straits give the Greeks the opportunity to control the frontage of an action, allowing their superior boarding skill full rein, while denying their more handy and swift opponents sea room to manoeuvre.

Instead of a board, the campaign I will now describe was in fact fought as a *map campaign*, using the Admiralty Chart 180 (AEGEAN SEA) as the basis. For convenience, this map was covered with a large sheet of Perspex, and the probable area of the land campaign was split up into mountainous terrain and plains, based on the physical map of Greece. The terrain was marked on the perspex sheet with a chinagraph pencil. The various areas of sea were similarly delineated, in this case by simply connecting up suitable headlands or islands to enclose a particular area. The illustration shows these areas for central Greece.

The question of troop representation was next considered. Here the method was that of the board wargame, with cardboard counters, $\frac{1}{2}$ in. square, to represent troop and fleet units. Red counters were cut from card for the Greek forces, and yellow for Xerxes' units, and the unit identification was inked on to them.

The actual size of unit represented by the counters was

based on an original contingent of 10,000 men. This not only fitted in well with the Persian 'myriad' system of army organisation, but also gave a fairly good approximation to the size of various Greek hoplite contingents. Equally, for the fleets, 10,000 men were the paper crews of 50 triremes, and therefore fleet counters representing 50 ships were in conformity with the scale.

Certain of the states of Greece were expected to change sides, e.g. the Thessalians, Boeotians and Argives. Equally, Xerxes had units in his forces which might have changed sides if circumstances had been right. The Macedonian forces were particularly likely to do so. For these units, two counters were prepared, one red and one yellow.

The counters finally prepared were as follows:

Force	Division	No. of Counters	Original size
Persian Fleet	Phoenician Fleet	4	200 ships approx
,,	Ionian Fleet	4	,,
,,	Egyptian Fleet	4	,,
,,	Cypriot Fleet	4	,,
Persian Army	Immortals	1	10,000 men approx
,,	Persians	1	,,
,,	Medes	1	,,
,,	Cissians	1	,,
,,	Hyrkanians	1	,,
,,	Other Subject Levies (unspecified)	10	100,000 men approx
,,	Persian cavalry	1	10,000 men approx
,,	Macedonians	1	,,
Greek Fleet	Athenians	4	200 ships approx
,,	Corinthians	1	50 ,, ,,
,,	Aeginetans	1	,, ,, ,,
,,	Allies	1	,, ,, ,,
Greek Armies	Thessalians (Cavalry)	1	10,000 men approx
,,	Boeotians	1	,,
,,	Athenians	1	,,
,,	Argives	1	,,
,,	Peloponnesians	1	,,
,,	Spartans	1	,,
,,	Leonidas' force	1	5,000 men approx

It will be noted that some simplification of the Greek fleet was necessary, with certain contingents being absorbed into the Corinthian and Aeginetan squadrons. The total number of counters was:

PERSIANS   *land*   27
               sea   16
                       43

GREEKS   *land*   7
               sea   7
                       14

This gave a reasonably realistic approximation to the historical odds.

To illustrate the rules under which the game was played out, a specimen game will be described, giving the various problems which were encountered, and the rules formulated to overcome them. This specimen game was interesting in that it followed quite closely the course of the original campaign, although, as will be seen, provision was made for an entirely different outcome.

The campaign was deemed to begin when the Persian army entered Thessaly, and so invaded free Greek territory.

The various Persian counters were disposed as follows:

All army units – north of the Olympus range
All fleet units – in the Thermaic Gulf

The Greek counters were nearly all based in their home areas, as follows:

Thessalians – Thessaly
Boeotians   – Boeotia
Athenians   – Attica
Argives   – Argos
Peloponnesian allies of Sparta – Arcadia
Spartans   – Laconia
Leonidas   – Thermopylae.

The Greek Fleet counters were all at Artemisium

except for one Athenian counter in the Chalcis narrows, and the Allies counter, which was at Pogon.

All these dispositions reflected the historical positions taken by the various units.

The first matter to settle, now that the counters had been disposed on the map, was the movement factor to be adopted. As a general rule, land units might be expected to move about 15–20 miles per day, and warships about 30. To calculate individual moves to this degree of accuracy would however involve each move consuming one day, and have made the game inconveniently long, with a three month campaign being stretched over nearly 100 moves. Since the campaign map had already been split up into areas, it was therefore decided simply to allow movement by any unit into an adjacent area, land units of course being restricted to land and sea units to sea – except where fleet units might transport troops. For the transport function, two fleet counters could convey one land counter *over a short distance* in one move – a short distance being from one land area to another across one sea area only, or perhaps two if the areas were narrow.

As an example of this transport movement, it would have required six Persian fleet counters to transport 30,000 troops across the Saronic Gulf from Attica to the Peloponnese south of the Isthmus.

The Persian supply fleet was not considered or included in the counters – the question of Persian supply will be dealt with later.

The Movement Rules so far devised permitted the Persian troops to enter Thessaly. Here of course they encountered a Greek unit, the Thessalians. It was determined that two or more units of opposing sides could not coexist in the same land or sea area of the map, and therefore either a battle must take place, or one side (in this case of course the Thessalians) change allegiance.

In the historical campaign the Thessalians changed sides immediately, and this was still the most likely course of events for them to follow. For the purposes of

147

the game, it was decided that a state might be expected to change sides under two circumstances – either when it was invaded by a Persian force, or when its troops had been defeated in a battle by the Persians. A table of probabilities was drawn up, showing the likelihood of each Greek state changing sides in these two eventualities. This table appeared as follows:

State	Dice score required to continue fighting On initial invasion	after defeat
THESSALY	6	6
BOEOTIA	5–6	5–6
ATHENS	(automatic fight)	2–6
ARGOS	4–6	4–6
SPARTA	(automatic fight)	(automatic fight)
PELOPONNESIANS	(automatic fight)	2–6

When the Persian army entered Thessaly, therefore, a die was thrown to see whether the Thessalians would resist. Although the probabilities were very much against this, nevertheless a six was thrown, meaning that the Thessalians fought the Persians.

The fighting was again settled by dice. The system adopted was that each class of troops was allocated a *combat factor*, and in a battle each side threw one die for each combat between units, the combat factors of the unit(s) involved in each side being added to the dice score. The combat factors were as follows:

Greek hoplite infantry counters : 4
Persian iron armoured infantry* or cavalry : 2
All other troops : 1

Similarly combat factors were allocated to fleet counters, as follows:

All Greek fleet units : 4
Phoenician, Egyptian & Cypriot fleet units : 2

---

* Persians, Medes, Cissians and Hyrkanians.

148

The number of counters which could be deployed in any battle was governed by the terrain. In open plains, or open sea, *all* the counters in the area could be brought to bear in a battle. In restricted areas, only as many units could be deployed as the *defender* chose to deploy units, and the combat factor of the attacking unit was halved.

Following a battle, the loser was forced to retreat out of of the area into an adjacent area, leaving the winner in possession. Counters could only be destroyed if defeated in presence of mobile enemies, who could press a pursuit. On land, this meant a cavalry counter, at sea, the Phoenician and Ionian fleets of Xerxes' Navy, and the Corinthian and Aeginetan squadrons of the Greek forces. In such cases, all units so defeated were considered destroyed. However, it was agreed that cavalry could escape from cavalry, and mobile fleet units from their opposite numbers, unless in a restricted area, or if surrounded.

In the case of the invasion of Thessaly, since the latter was an open plain, the Persians could deploy their entire forces, and the Thessalians thus had no hope of defeating them. After an initial battle, therefore, the Thessalians again threw to see if they changed sides, which this time occurred. The red counter was thereupon removed, and the Thessalians, represented by a yellow counter, joined Xerxes' army.

The Persian army now moved foward to the plain of Lamia, facing the Thermopylae position held by Leonidas and his men. Meanwhile the Persian fleet also moved down opposite the Artemisium position.

At this point further restrictions on movement were called into being. Historically, the Persians were extremely short of anchorage space. Therefore the number of ships which they could keep in the area of the Gulf of Volos, opposite the Greeks at Artemisium, was limited to four Fleet counters, with the rest having to be based in the area of Cape Sepeia.

In addition, at this stage, Rules were required to cover both the weather and the supply problem facing the

Persians. Supply first: it was decided that the Persian army would suffer attrition by one myriad of 10,000 men for every turn of the game after the seventh in which the army or part of it was not in an area adjacent to at least one friendly fleet counter. Since the Gulf of Volos was adjacent to Thessaly, and Thessaly adjacent to the Plain of Lamia, these conditions were not met, and the Persians had only seven tries to break through the Greek defence before the army would start losing men through hunger, or have to retreat back into Thessaly.

Weather rules, intended to reproduce the effect of the storm which struck the Persian fleet, were adopted as follows: on every game turn a die should be thrown, and if a six came up, then a northeasterly storm broke out, and any fleet unit not in a sheltered area would have to throw four to six on the dice to survive. The storm would then continue until a further six was thrown.

The Persian fleet tactics and strategy were exactly as in the original historical campaign. The Phoenician fleet moved into the Gulf of Volos, and 200 ships (2 × Egyptian & 2 × Cypriot counters) were sent south to try to outflank the Greeks and come up the Euripus from the South. The remainder of the fleet units were off Cape Sepeia.

The course of the conflict can now be conveniently described in game turns. In the course of Game Turn one the Persian Immortals were sent in to attack the Spartans in the Thermopylae pass, and there was an engagement between two Egyptian Fleet counters and the Aeginetan and one Athenian Fleet counter off Cape Sepeia. Since the area was held to constitute narrow waters, only two Persian counters could oppose the two Greek counters played.

The result of the fighting was that the Immortals were hurled back from the pass, and the Egyptian fleet units were defeated. Since they were defeated in the presence of a fast unit, namely the Aeginetans, these two fleet units were destroyed.

No storm ensued in this period on the dice throw.

Second Period. The dice throw indicated that a storm had broken, and all exposed Persian fleet counters had to dice. As a result, two of the Ionian fleet counters off Cape Sepeia were lost, and the whole of the flanking force, now off southern Euboea, was destroyed. This was a remarkable dice throw, in that it reproduced almost exactly the course of the original campaign.

The Persian fleet was now reduced to the following strength: four Phoenician counters, two Ionian counters, and two Cypriot counters. The odds had therefore been very much evened up.

In the meantime the Persian army had again tried to storm the pass, and failed, not surprisingly because of the difference in odds!

Of course, facing the Thermopylae position, it was to be expected that the Persians would try to find a way round. A Rule was made that as from the second period of play in front of the Thermopylae position, they could throw one die each turn. A throw of six would mean the flanking route round had been betrayed to them or found. Once this occurred, the Persians could deploy a second counter against Leonidas' single counter, and would no longer have their combat factors halved. It was also decided that deployment of a second Persian counter would mean that if Leonidas were defeated, he would be surrounded, and destroyed.

For the third, fourth and fifth Periods of play, the storm continued to rage so there was no naval activity, while the Persians continued to make unavailing frontal attacks on the Thermopylae position.

At the start of the Sixth Period, the storm died away, and in addition, the pass was betrayed to the Persians. The result was as in the historical campaign – Leonidas was surrounded and wiped out.

In the meantime a large naval battle was fought between the Greek and Persian fleets, now more nearly equal in number. The engagements between the separate components of the fleet were fought separately, with the combat being indecisive, except for the loss of one Athenian fleet counter, defeated by a mobile Phoenician one.

At the end of this period of play, the Greeks retired from the Artemisium position, and the Persians moved forward to occupy it. This brought fleet units back in contact with the Persian army, and just averted the threatened famine impending for Xerxes' army.

This concluded the battle for the Thermopylae/Artemisium line, which had corresponded remarkably well with the original campaign.

The Persians now moved forward into Boeotia – and a dice throw showed that the Boeotians immediately went over to Xerxes, and a yellow counter replaced the red. The Persian army moved forward again into Attica, and the fleet into the Eastern Saronic Gulf.

In the meantime, the Greek fleet had all mustered in the Salamis strait, and the Athenian army was also at Salamis, on the island. The remainder of the Greek land forces held the line of the Isthmus of Corinth, with the exception of the Argives, who were still in their own home territory. After the defeat of Leonidas (or the seventh day of the attack on Thermopylae, whichever was sooner) all Greek units so far uncommitted (except the Argives) were permitted to move from their original positions.

The strategic situation was now that prevailing just before the battle of Salamis. The Persian land army was in Attica and the fleet was in support of them, occupying the East Saronic Gulf. While the army was intact, the fleet had so far lost a total of eight counters, or half its strength, in the series of battles and storms at Artemisium. The fleet thus had only eight counters, while the Greek fleet still had six available, as the Athenian unit lost at Artemisium had been made up by the Allied counter from Pogon. The Athenian land forces counter was on the island of Salamis. Of the other Greek land forces counters, the Argives were still neutral, the Thessalians and Boeotians had changed sides, and Leonidas and his force had been destroyed. Only the Laconian counter itself and the Peloponnesian Allies counter remained, and these units were placed in the Isthmus of Corinth.

The strategic situation was in effect a stalemate, if the Greeks made no move. The Persian army could not move forward into the Megarid to threaten the Isthmus of Corinth, because this defence line, occupied by twice Leonidas' strength, was as strong as the Thermopylae line, and they would, as at Thermopylae, be outrunning their supply lines, and could not maintain a presence for more than seven days. More important, there was no possibility, in assaulting the Isthmus, of finding a secret pass which would enable additional force to be brought to bear on the defenders. Using the fleet to transport troops would not be possible, because ships carrying troops would lose all their combat factors, under a rule designed to simulate the handicap such troop-carrying vessels would have been under in real life. This ruled out either an assault against the island of Salamis – which in any case was strongly defended – or a landing on the other side of the Saronic Gulf, e.g. near Pogon.

The only offensive action which the Persians could therefore take was a direct assault against the Greek fleet in the Salamis strait. This was on the understanding that the Greek unity did not collapse and the fleet attempt to break out and escape.

To reproduce the effect of these two possibilities, it was decided to throw one die for the Greeks and another for the Persians six times, representing an estimated six remaining weeks of the campaigning season left before Xerxes would have to retire. If the Persian die (thrown first) was one or two, it would mean that the Persians would attempt to enter the strait (or be induced to enter by the Greek deception plan). If the Greek die was a one, it would mean that they would attempt to break out and retire to the Isthmus. If this happened, they would in fact succeed, probably, in moving into the west Saronic Gulf area, but this would then allow the Persian army to advance to the Megarid, and the Persian fleet to engage an outnumbered and outclassed Greek fleet in open waters.

In fact, after two periods of play, the Persians threw a two, which meant that they attempted to enter the straits. They had four Phoenician, two Ionian, and two Cypriot units, whose normal combat factors of two, four and two respectively were reduced, because they were attacking in narrow waters, to one, two and one. Opposing them were six Greek counters, three Athenian, one Aeginetan, one Corinthian and one Allied, all with a combat factor of four.

Reproducing the original strategic disposition, the Persians sent the two Cypriot counters to the western end of the straits, while the remaining fleet units were committed to the eastern strait. Again reproducing the original dispositions, the Greeks sent the Corinthians to the western exit, while the rest of their units were facing the Persian attack on the eastern end.

Since the Greeks were only in possession of five counters in the eastern strait, the Persians were compelled by the rules to deploy only this number of counters against them also. Three Phoenician counters and two Ionian counters were deployed.

Under the fighting rules, giving a heavy advantage to the Greek defenders of the straits, only one Persian unit had sufficient dice score to defeat an opposite number; as the winning unit was a mobile Phoenician one, the Greek counter (allied) was destroyed. However, all the other Greek counters were victorious, and since there was a mobile unit (Aeginetan) present, these defeated units were also destroyed.

The final losses therefore in the map game described here were four Persian counters, representing 200 ships, and one Greek counter, representing 50 ships. These losses are quite close to the losses which it is estimated each side sustained in the original action.

Following this battle the position of the Persians in the map campaign was now hopeless, and their remaining three fleet units were inferior in numbers and mobility to the survivors of the Greek fleet, who had five units, two of which were mobile (Aeginetan and Corinthian). Both Persian army and fleet therefore retreated, and the Greeks had won the campaign.

At this point the map campaign was terminated, since it was being fought primarily as a background to the naval engagements, and in particular Salamis. It would however have been a simple matter, using the same counters, to have fought the campaign of the following year, in which the Greek land forces defeated the Persian troops left behind by Xerxes. To represent this, the Greek forces should comprise the Athenian, Spartan and Allied counters, while the Persian forces will include the Immortals, one other Persian counter (infantry) and the Persian cavalry, together with the Boeotian infantry and Thessalian cavalry units.

Whilst the basic methods and rules of this map campaign are very simple, they are capable of being elaborated to any degree of complexity, and they give a reasonably accurate background to the campaign for the wargamer seeking to fight individual aspects of it in greater detail. It has not been possible to give the detail of every rule used in the description of the campaign, and not every contingency has been covered. However, anyone replaying it on his own account will easily be able to fill in the details for himself by reference to what actually happened, or might have happened, in the original campaign of 480 B.C.

Appendix
References and Sources
for Models

1. Written sources

This present work is not one in which it is possible to refer constantly in the text to authorities, or to give a full bibliography. A partial bibliography follows, and the works cited are up to date, so that the reader wishing to follow any further points will be able to use the works cited (which were not the only ones consulted) as a starting point for his enquiries.

The bibliography may be split as follows:

Ancient Sources:

HERODOTUS: *History*. Herodotus is the main ancient historian for the Persian war, and numerous versions of his *History* are available in translation, including one in the 'Penguin Classics' series. For readers with ancient Greek who prefer to have a translation readily available, the Loeb Classical library (4 vols) version is convenient. Salamis is in the 4th volume.

Herodotus was not an eyewitness of the battle, but obtained his facts from veterans, probably on both sides.

AESCHYLUS: *The Persians*. Aeschylus wrote his tragedy *The Persians* within eight years of the battle, in which he himself fought as a marine in the Athenian fleet. It takes place in

Persia, and a series of long set speeches from a messenger sets out for the old men left at home the disaster which overtook Xerxes. There is thus a long verse narrative describing the battle, supposedly from the Persian side. OTHER SOURCES: There are details in Plutarch's *Lives of Themistocles* and *Aristides*, and an account in the historian Diodorus Siculus.

Modern Sources:
On the Campaign and the Battle:
A. R. BURN: *Persia and the Greeks*, the Defence of the West 546–478 B.C., Arnold 1962. This book covers the whole era, with the Persian Wars as its centre piece.
C. HIGNETT: *Xerxes Invasion of Greece*. Oxford University Press, 1963. The emphasis of this book is on discussion of the various theories put forward by scholars to make sense of the battle and of the various other problems involved.
P. GREEN: *The Year of Salamis*. Weidenfeld & Nicolson, 1970. Written by a classical scholar who is also a first class historical novelist and resident in Greece, this book is good on the terrain and personalities involved. It covers not only Salamis but the remainder of the campaign, as its title suggests.

The above three books contain full scholarly apparatus.

On Ancient Naval Warfare and Ships:
MORRISON AND WILLIAMS: *Greek Oared Ships 900–322 B.C.* 1968. This is a comprehensive survey of all the available evidence relating to the trireme and other ancient warships.
R. C. ANDERSON: *Oared Fighting Ships*. Percival Marshall, 1962. Covers the whole range of galley warfare up to the 18th Century.
R. B. NELSON: *Warfleets of Antiquity*. Wargames Research Group, 1973. Covers ancient ship types and campaigns; an earlier work by the present author.

On Ancient Naval Wargaming and Rules:
D. F. FEATHERSTONE: *Naval Wargames*. Stanley Paul, 1965. Contains a chapter written with the cooperation of Tony Bath and setting out his ancient naval rules.
E. P. SMITH: *Greek Naval Warfare*. London Wargames

Section. This contains the Rules written by Ed Smith.
R. B. NELSON: *Naval Wargame Rules*. Wargames Research
Group, 1973. The rules in the present book are modified and
condensed variants of these rules, which cover all ancient
naval warfare.
Periodicals :
Slingshot : The Journal of the Society of Ancients is published by the Society six times a year and is the only periodical
exclusively devoted to Ancient wargaming.

2. Maps

First class maps are essential for following an historical
campaign, and fortunately for naval battles Admiralty
Charts are of very considerable use. The following charts
are valuable for Salamis and the rest of the Campaign:
Admiralty Chart 180 : Aegean Sea
This covers the entire Aegean at a scale of 1:1,100,000 and
conveniently gives the whole area of the campaign.
Admiralty Chart 1556 : Gulf of Volos
This is a large scale chart which covers the whole area of the
Artemisium/Thermopylae action at a scale of 1:109,000 or
about 1½ miles to the inch. This chart is particularly useful
in that the contours and layout of the ground near the coasts
is shown.
Admiralty Chart 1657 : Saronikos Kolpos
This shows the island of Salamis and the whole surrounding
area on a scale of 1:100,000. Again the contours of land are
shown.

3. Ships

The ancient naval wargamer is somewhat poorly served for
suitable ship models of accurate type. 1:1200 model ships
are, to the author's knowledge, produced by:
Skytrex Ltd.,
28 Church St.,
Wymeswold,
Loughborough,
Leicestershire.
Skytrex also produce a range of other wargaming accessories
and can supply both the Author's rules and the London
Wargame's Section's Rules. The former may alternatively
be obtained direct from:
Wargames Research Group,
75 Ardingley Drive,
Goring by Sea,
Sussex.

Index

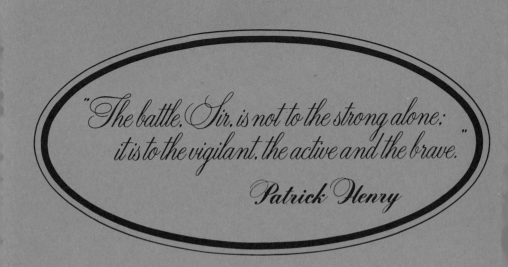

"The battle, Sir, is not to the strong alone:
it is to the vigilant, the active and the brave."

Patrick Henry